# WITH THE ROYAL TANK REGIMENT IN KOREA

*For Dumpy*
*and dedicated to former, current and future members of the extended Royal Tank Regiment family.*
*Fear Naught*

# WITH THE ROYAL TANK REGIMENT IN KOREA

## CENTURIONS ON THE HOOK

JIM SELWAY

Pen & Sword
MILITARY
AN IMPRINT OF PEN & SWORD BOOKS LTD.
YORKSHIRE – PHILADELPHIA

First published in Great Britain in 2025 by
Pen & Sword Military
An imprint of
Pen & Sword Books Ltd
Yorkshire – Philadelphia



ISBN 978 1 39903 846 1



A CIP catalogue record for this book is available from the British Library.



Typeset by SJmagic DESIGN SERVICES, India.

Printed and bound in the UK by CPI Group (UK) Ltd.

The Publisher's authorised representative in the EU for product safety is Authorised Rep Compliance Ltd., Ground Floor, 71 Lower Baggot Street, Dublin D02 P593, Ireland.
www.arccompliance.com

For a complete list of Pen & Sword titles please contact

PEN & SWORD BOOKS LIMITED
George House, Units 12 & 13, Beevor Street, Off Pontefract Road,
Barnsley, South Yorkshire, S71 1HN, England
E-mail: enquiries@pen-and-sword.co.uk
Website: www.pen-and-sword.co.uk

or

PEN AND SWORD BOOKS
1950 Lawrence Rd, Havertown, PA 19083, USA
E-mail: uspen-and-sword@casematepublishers.com
Website: www.penandswordbooks.com

# Contents

# Foreword

*By Brigadier Gavin Thompson, Colonel Commandant, The Royal Tank Regiment, 2023*

When I joined H Squadron, 1st Royal Tank Regiment in 1994, the then commanding officer set the subalterns of my squadron the task of researching the Regiment's contribution to the Korean War to create a display board. Most of that research came from Volume 3 of 'The Tanks'.

The author, the late Major Ken Macksey MC, focussed his attention on the tactics and equipment employed. Through anecdotes and the stories that

Brigadier Gavin Thompson.

emerge from the fog of war, Jim Selway brings a new human richness to the regiment's history in Korea. Delighting equally in what went well through design and the success that emerged through pure good fortune and shining his light onto the wonderful characters with whom he served, Jim Selway is as well qualified as anyone to comment having successfully proved himself under characters such as Major, later General, Sir Richard Ward, DSO and Bar, MC, Croix du Guerre, Croix du Leopold.

This book tells of the awe in which the veterans of World War 2 were held by the post war generation, the close bonds of trust and loyalty within tank crews and the deep respect, often expressed through humour, between tanks and infantry. It also gives a human feel for the early Cold War conditions in the British Army of the Rhine.

There is some truth in Jim's reflection that Korea was a forgotten war. The Royal Tank Regiment keeps the spirit alive. Each year, on Korea Day, the Regiment rings the Korea Bell. The bell is forged from brass shells fired in that war. In this 70th anniversary year, Jim's stories are a timely addition to our understanding of that war, the people who served in it and the British Army of its time.

# Introduction

I make no apology for submitting this little history to the public following the 70th anniversary of the signing of the truce that effectively ended the Korean War. Far too little is known or appreciated about that war, fought between 1950 and 1953, and its critical impact. Put simply, if the United Nations had not reacted to North Korea's Russian and Chinese-led war, the whole of what we call the Far East would now in all probability be under communist governments.

Additionally, no one has yet written as an 'insider' of the valuable and highly praised contribution the 1st Royal Tank Regiment made during the last 8 months of that war. Sadly, it appears that in 2023 I am the last surviving officer who fought with the Regiment in Korea and thus am proud to have the opportunity of mentioning some of those who contributed to that success and who deserve to have their names and exploits recorded for posterity.

Captain James Selway, 1st and 3rd Royal Tank Regiment.

For sure, it was one of the bitterest wars ever fought. Thus, I hope this book not only throws some further light on what has so unfairly become a 'Forgotten War' but helps record the highly successful role my own Regiment – The 1st Royal Tank Regiment-played in holding back the massive assaults of the Chinese on the United Nations' lines, and does great credit to those who fought them off.

# INTRODUCTION

The motto of the Royal Tank Regiment is 'Fear Naught' and I like to think this book will show how my Regiment lived up to it despite the massive efforts made by the Chinese in what the highly respected author and former Gunner Troop Commander, Brigadier Brian Parritt, so vividly described in his autobiographical book on the Korean War, 'Chinese Hordes and Human Waves'.

Finally, Part One of this memoir hopes to convey the general experience of serving in a tank regiment during this last phase of the Korean War and during the Cold War in the 1950s, rather than a blow-by-blow account. The Regiment's record in Korea is well documented and chronological accounts of its deployment are available from many other sources. A précis appears in the Regiment's Korean Journal (in Appendix B) which was written by me at the time when my memories and those of my fellow contributors were fresh and this official record was endorsed by the commanding structure that oversaw the events described.

Part Two describes the typical life of a Tank Regiment officer serving in the Cold War army and hopes to outline the array of experiences that we were offered.

Above all, this memoir focuses on the people we were privileged to live and work with and the lifelong bonds that Army service forged.

Fear Naught<br>JAS. Lower Shockerwick, near Bath, 2024

## PART ONE

# THROUGH THE MUD AND BLOOD...

### A Young Officer's Experiences and the Korean War

Overlooking the Chinese positions from my Centurion on the Hook.

# Prelude

# A Young Officer's Experiences

The 1st Royal Tank Regiment had been detailed for active service in Korea in support of the Commonwealth Division with effect from December 1952. We were to relieve the 5th Royal Inniskilling Dragoon Guards (the Skins) and take over their Mark III Centurion Tanks already in battle positions on the front line. These positions were established by 7 RTR in 1951 with Churchill flamethrowing tanks and then passed to the 8th Irish Hussars who had passed them to the Skins. The Mark III Cents were Britain's latest tank and probably the most effective tank in the world at that time.

2nd Lt James Selway. 1 RTR. Freshly commissioned subaltern from Sandhurst 1949, aged 20.

On that cold windy night, the night before the regiment set out on their journey across the seas, I was trying hard to appear cool and nonchalant. I had missed serving in the Second World War by a whisker but had spent the previous 4 years training for this opportunity and now I was apprehensive. I had attended the Royal Military Academy Sandhurst in 1947 and was commissioned into the Royal Tank Regiment in July 1949 at a 'passing out' parade held in front of Princess Elizabeth, as she was then. I think I was in a minority for not appreciating Sandhurst's value in preparing young officers. I deplored the lack of specific training in actually commanding soldiers and in basic tactics, or indeed map reading. It wasn't

The Guard Room at Hobart Barracks, Detmold. The Regimental Police were very tough on everyone, even the officers!!

until I was posted to Bovington Camp in Dorset and received some initial training on tanks, that I felt I was really beginning to learn about soldiering. Indeed, I felt those who obtained commissions through the much shorter Mons OCTU course and joined their regiments sooner, learned to command troops faster than academy graduates!

Although Sandhurst was almost exclusively staffed by officers and NCOs who had distinguished themselves in WW2, the academy still focused on drill and the technical and theoretical doctrine that pre-war textbooks and training schedules still promoted. Nearly all the instructors were articulate, experienced and inspiring and had more up to date ideas on warfare that were suppressed by the Academy's pre-war curriculum. I would have given anything to be lectured on war and man management by these battle experienced men instead. Ultimately, a month with the Regiment did more to prepare me for what to expect in war and the best way to motivate soldiers to do what you wanted without shouting at them or resorting to the law than two years at Sandhurst.

My father had served with the Artist's Rifles as an infantry officer in France during the First World War but as a cadet I had become particularly interested in tank warfare and hoped for a future in the Royal Armoured Corps. Selection for the RTR was highly competitive and gloriously, through the wonderful support and encouragement of Captain Paul Tapsell, the Royal Tank Regiment's representative, I joined the 1st Tanks, based in Germany, after commissioning. From that moment, life took on a wonderful new purpose and I started to learn what was needed to be an officer.

The regiment was part of the new NATO force located in defensive positions along the Rhine, ready to hold out against a possible Soviet attack. We took our role very seriously and on arrival I was immediately sent on 'Battle Training Exercises'. I was fortunately among the first batch of Royal Armoured Corps officers who only ever trained and fought on the new Centurion tank.

The Centurion was introduced shortly after the Second World War and in terms of manoeuvrability, firepower, survivability and communications, was far ahead of the Warsaw Pact equipment it was designed to face.

Except as a Prefect at school, at no time in my life had I commanded men, let alone a tank troop. To get experience, my squadron leader handed me over to a highly experienced Sergeant, Spike Mason, who had fought with the regiment all the way from El Alamein to Berlin. Spike was given the task of knocking me into shape to become an effective Troop Commander. With astonishing respect and patience, he suggested that I be his tank 'gunner' on that first particular exercise. As I watched through the gunner's periscope sight and listened on the radio to his instructions to his crew and to the crews manning the other tanks in the troop of four, I began to learn what was required of a troop leader.

These 'exercises' took place on enormous plains in Northern Germany where the British Army would be split into two with one half attacking the other. The exercises often lasted for several weeks. At the end of each day, members of the troop erected 'lean-to' tents against the side of the tanks whilst others brewed up a meal. It was during those meals that I really started to learn about soldiering.

Nearly all the men had fought in the war and sitting around the evening 'bivvis', talk invariably shifted from our performance in the day's exercises and ended by reminiscing about exploits in the war and the leadership of various officers and tank commanders. What was astonishing was the loyalty of the soldiers. Unlike Mark Anthony's claim that 'the evil that men

Detmold. The REME workshops, training station and vehicle park. When not on exercise, most of our day was spent here.

do lives after them, the good is oft interred in their bones', these soldiers reminisced about the exploits of their bosses. They would very, very rarely be critical and if they were it was in a fatherly way. Instinctively as a young trainee officer I began to learn what led these men into a battle. Put simply it was 'example'. Thus, when over 50 years later, one of my former soldiers in Korea wrote on his Facebook wall that I had 'led my troop by example' I could not help but feel immensely proud to have received what I considered to be the highest accolade.

It is perhaps well worth recalling here that at this time every officer in the regiment over the rank of Lieutenant had secured significant battle experience in the war. A glance at any picture of the regiment's officers in 1950 shows them all wearing impressive rows of medals. This wealth of experience might have restricted the exposure of younger officers to command experience but contributed to the success and safety of our mission.

But here I would like to mention that one key purpose of this story is to tell the world of the marvellous comradeship shown within tank crews. It was no good saying 'I'm an officer, I don't cook the meals'. If your four man crew were tightening a loose tank track or loading heavy fuel cans, the officer did his bit and lost no respect in doing it. Tank crews earned the reputation of being a 'Band of Brothers'. All four of our lives depended on each of us pulling together. I owe much to my crews, all of whom supported me superbly, both in actual battle in Korea and regimental life in general.

Over the two years after joining the 'First' in 1949, I became more confident and competent at handling tanks in mock battles, and proficient at the more routine tasks of barrack life. Without doubt the highlight of those years was exercises where there were few limits on scale or costs. On reflection 70 years later, I realise how fortunate we were with 'budgets'. If you wanted to drive your tanks for 50 miles, you could and no one questioned the cost! What is called 'Track Mileage' was immaterial except to know when replacement tank tracks were needed. If you want to upset a modern troop commander, just tell him that and ask him how many track miles he is allowed!!

In Detmold we had a superb purpose-built officers' mess which included a magnificent dining room complete with minstrels' gallery, set halfway down the room. Field Marshal Herman Göring had visited often and addressed student cadets from this lofty lookout but, in our day, the

The Commanding Officer Lt Col Peter Sturdee inspects the Regiment outside Hobart Barracks in Germany in the early 50s. Note the awards on the officers, the RSM and NCOs. The shoulder flash of the WW1 Mark IV tank remains a regimental tradition.

Regimental band used it for its intended purpose, entertaining us from on high during major dinner nights.

When I joined the Regiment in Detmold in 1949, the Officers' Mess was run by excellent German staff under a mess steward called Charlie. He relished his role and kindly claimed he preferred looking after us compared to the Luftwaffe Air Force cadets for whom our barracks had been built. There was little he wouldn't do for the mess members, for instance in the middle of a long dinner night, when leaving the table was not permitted until after the toasts, he might approach a seated officer and discreetly pass an empty bottle – and collect it, equally discreetly, three minutes later. Charlie's paternal attitude typified the postwar Germans' lack of hostility or resentment to the allied forces posted there and many soldiers married German women, although officers were forbidden to marry Germans until well into the 1950s. World peace would be easily secured if every bachelor Brit should be required to marry a foreigner! Britain could never go to war with a country which had so many 'foreign' mothers-in-law!

In the 1940s and 50s, military wives rarely took civilian jobs and so participated much more in regimental life. The soldiers' wives were often very young, lonely and homesick and the officers' wives felt a responsibility to support them. This normally included solving domestic problems which, more often than not, were matters of pregnancy. For the families, the officers' wives made sure they received the treatment they needed and

1 RTR Officers. Detmold c1950. Sadly I was on leave and not included. They could have made another Centurion tank if they melted down their medals but the experience was worth more than another squadron in the line.

arranged for someone to look after older siblings when their mother went into labour. For the subalterns, the wives provided first class intel on the state of morale in the regiment and likely trouble spots to steer clear of.

Most Sundays the mess hosted pre-lunch drinks parties for the wives and children, a ritual that was huge fun. The more junior subalterns drew the short straws and were required to look after the children, usually outside in the mess garden, while their more established colleagues enjoyed the party.

At Christmas time, the married officers hosted the unmarried subalterns to festive lunches in their houses. They used to compete against each other to send their guests back to the mess suitably inebriated and publicly enthusiastic about the charm and culinary skills of the wife who had hosted them. Those were memorable Christmases!!

Alongside normal duties, I was sent off for a six-month posting to Brigade Headquarters to fulfil the role of Regimental Liaison Officer, which included responsibility for the 50 or more transport vehicles allocated to Brigade HQ. This was a valuable training posting bringing me into almost daily contact with the highly respected Brigadier David Belchem, who had excelled as one of Field Marshall Montgomery's bright and personable Staff officers. He finished his career as a General but while at Brigade HQ he taught me a lot and gave me much encouragement, especially when I reacted to his comment that his Command Vehicle – a variation of a 3 ton lorry – was too slow and cumbersome.

To overcome his complaint, I got the HQ fitters to convert his ordinary Jeep into a mobile command post, utilising its massive cross country ability. On special platforms, we fitted two radio sets built with extra long aerials – one connecting him to the regiments under his command and the other to divisional headquarters. Much of the time he chose to drive himself and on exercises it was wonderful to see him hurling this vehicle at steep slopes with a flash of his 'churning' arms whilst carrying out the multiple tasks of steering, changing gears, attacking the challenging hills or banks, ordering his regiments to implement his instructions and keeping his divisional commander in the picture. He went on to be a Divisional commander himself during the time I was posted to Korea.

I was away from Germany on a technical course at Bovington Camp in Dorset in June 1952 when I got a message that 'the 1st Royal Tanks' were to relieve the Skins (the 5th Inniskilling Dragoon Guards) in Korea that coming December and that we would be sailing by troopship from Britain in October. This meant that the Regiment would leave Germany, having served there continuously since the day it crossed the German frontier at the head of 21 Army Group in the rush to Berlin. I returned to Germany and helped the Regiment prepare to hand over the barracks to our replacements in the line.

As a regiment, we assembled in Tidworth in September 1952 with a few weeks to prepare before we embarked on a troopship at the end of October to sail for Korea. I was posted to command 3 Troop, 'B' Squadron and we conducted final training exercises on Salisbury Plain with our new commanders. That is when butterflies in my stomach began to stir! My new boss was to be the most decorated soldier I had ever met and indeed was ever to meet, Major Richard Ward, DSO and Bar, MC, Croix du Guerre, Croix du Leopold, with a reputation as a strict taskmaster that matched his fighting record in the North African desert against Rommel and later in France. 'Dick' Ward had perhaps more influence on my life than any other. His standards were always totally uncompromising. He did what he considered to be the correct action and you followed. To stray from this path was not to be recommended.

In Korea as I got to know him better, I asked him one night why and when he developed these uncompromisingly high standards and his answer got to the bottom of soldiering and his philosophy. In the desert in WW2, he had commanded a troop of tanks that had been involved for three days and nights in the bloody 'Cauldron' battle. He was then pulled out of the battle and sent into reserve many miles behind the front line.

On arrival, he told his exhausted crews to dig slit trenches and then crash out.

His sergeant had argued that they were 20 miles behind the frontline, the men were exhausted and it was safe to get some sleep. Much against his better judgement, Dick Ward gave way and that night they were overrun by the Germans. Only he and a handful escaped capture or death and he vowed that this could never be allowed to happen again. It is why he built his astonishing reputation for uncompromising decisions which commanded total respect. He always went to great pains to brief everybody fully and carefully so they knew exactly where they stood. It became clear too that he valued everyone's life and was not going to risk anyone needlessly.

These standards explain why he was so highly trusted and admired. 'Fierce' but highly respected, he led by example.

The following spring when the regiment was stationed on the Suez Canal in Egypt, the time came for him to move on. I had by now been promoted to Squadron second in command and it fell to me to select the traditional leaving present. I must admit to being quite anxious about asking the soldiers to subscribe. After all, there were still 3 former sergeants in the squadron who he had reduced to the ranks as well as Troopers he had punished for not being up to standard. I needn't have worried though for every soldier in the Squadron, including the 3 sergeants, contributed to the gift. Not one of them bore him any ill will. Their respect for him and his decisions was total. The gift I selected was a model of a Korean Torre (an arched gateway suspending a large bell) and 20 years later I was delighted to see it still being used on his dinner table in the UK and later after his rather early death, by one of his daughters to summon the family to the table!

Major 'Dick' Ward, later General Sir Richard Ward (Left) with the author in Gloucester Valley, Korea. 1953.

Some years later, I learned of another incredible example of his leadership. In 1957, long after the Korean War, I had joined him while he was commanding the 3 RTR in Detmold in Germany. He had given me the plum appointment of commanding the Recce (Reconnaissance) Troop, the eyes of the regiment; each man handpicked. Their task was to fan out in two man 'Scout Cars' ahead of the regiment and direct the tanks to effective battle positions or provide early warning of approaching enemy. This required above average intelligence from each soldier as well as great map reading skills. To develop these skills, I requested permission to 'hatch up' with the commander of the Recce Troop of the nearby Skins (The Royal Inniskilling Dragoon Guards) for a joint exercise in the American zone of Germany. Since this area was normally out of bounds without explicit authority, navigating here would really test the map reading skills of the scout car commanders. Both Colonel Mike Tomkin of the Skins and Dick Ward agreed to it but the night before we set off, our adjutant discovered that Rhine Army permission was needed 3 weeks ahead for any British troops entering the American zone. Dick Ward took the decision that it was

A small dent that might have had international repercussions! The accident occurred in the US Zone and we had not sought permission to be there.

a valuable, well-planned exercise and that we should go, but exhorted me to ensure there were no traffic accidents as these would be sure to come to the attention of the American authorities.

We set off, but right in the centre of Heidelberg one of my Scout cars was involved in a collision that secured newspaper headlines and a picture in the local German press. Although the paper pleasingly praised the British driver for skilfully avoiding a much more serious accident and not injuring civilians, it was exactly the attention we were hoping to avoid. On my return I reported the incident to Colonel Dick who dismissed it as 'one of those things' and I heard no more about it. Many years later I was mentioning this story to another retired army chum. He told me he was posted to Army Headquarters at the time and was aware of Dick Ward being summoned before the Army Commander. He had been threatened with a Court Martial but the case was dropped. What was so remarkable about that story was that he never told me. I'm not so sure that a lesser man would have stayed silent on my behalf.

Later still in 2022, I received the following tribute to Dick Ward from a squadron colleague, John Nolan (who was a corporal in Korea and appears later in my chapter on the battles of the Hook):

> *Before Dick Ward finally relinquished command of B Squadron while in the Canal Zone, he made it known that he would attend the NAAFI at a specific time to enable the other ranks to say goodbye. The squaddies turned out in large numbers, including some uninvited members of other Squadrons, one of whom, in loud and foul language, made known his objections to our Squadron Commander. It wasn't long before there was a distinct 'thump' followed by a 'thud' and the sound of severe retching: QED: Any comments, within reason, were acceptable but only from B Squadron members, not the roughs and scruffs of the unmentionables.*
>
> *I spoke with him, wished him well and he commented favourably on my promotion to corporal.*
>
> *He always reminded me of a teacher, an austere figure, strict but fair. His observation to the U.S. 1st Marine Division's staff when they took over our sector of the line in Korea, on where*

*the enemy were forming and where their main thrust would come from, was given in a dry, methodical and convincing manner, so typical of the man for whom I always had the highest respect.*

Dick went on to be Army Commander in the Far East and in 1971, as a civilian, I visited him in the lovely 'Flagstaff House' in Hong Kong. I was not surprised to see that there and later still in the second top job in the War Office, he had lost none of his reputation as a stickler for perfection! In WW2, he was awarded more medals for bravery than anyone else I knew.

A fellow officer in 1 RTR, Micky Farmer, praised Dick Ward's prudence in challenging a proposed, but potentially rash, action against the Chinese:

*The question of a possible armoured raid cropped up again. I can remember Major Ward and me sitting in an OP on the forward slopes of Point 159 discussing it. I was foolishly, but I suppose understandably, hoping the troop chosen to do it would be mine. He was not enthusiastic and told me that he was going to advise the Commanding Officer and if possible the Divisional Commander as well, that such an operation was not on. He said that the possible gains would be of little value and would certainly be outweighed by the risks to men and vehicles.*

He had seen too many people lost in the war on operations which were not absolutely essential. Now Major Ward's experience as a tank soldier was second to none and his exploits were legendary. Accordingly, his advice was taken and indeed we heard no more about the proposed armoured raid. I have always remembered that conversation because, had Major Ward been an officer with an undistinguished war record or none at all, he might well have felt that honour demanded that he should show himself to be keen for action and to show a good aggressive spirit, even if in his heart he doubted the wisdom of the operation. In which case quite possibly, unnecessary casualties might have been suffered to no worthwhile purpose.

Although I (and my colleagues) felt we were sharper now than ever before, virtually everything we did or said met with sharp criticism. In his first few

Micky Farmer, a fellow troop commander in B Squadron, proposed a fighting patrol against a Chinese position to Dick Ward. Mickey Farmer and I went on leave to Japan together whilst we were stationed in Korea.

days with us, Dick Ward made us all feel unworthy of our positions. When we were sent on embarkation leave, I don't think any of us were confident that we were going to be fit to command to his standards. With this in mind, we all returned from leave somewhat subdued and fearing the worst.

On the night before we were due to sail to Korea, I was having a quiet drink in the mess when I was called behind the bar to see Corporal Goldie, my troop corporal. When I faced him, he said,

'Sir, I thought I ought to tell you, the troops are muttering uneasily'. Did I want to go and see them? Drawing myself up to my full height I answered as would be expected of any leader facing mutiny.

'Yes of course.' What else could I do? Go to bed and put my pillow over my head?

We set out in ominous silence across a dark, rainswept and windy square to the troops hut. Why I wondered did it have to be me who had a mutinous troop and what would Major Ward have to say in the morning? Life seemed very cruel and I recall Corporal Goldie interrupting my thoughts to ask me again on the doorstep of the hut if I still wanted to go in? Doing my best to give the impression that I was completely in control, I repeated tersely 'Yes, of course' and he flung the door open. Confronting me were my 14 soldiers sitting on their beds, sullenly cleaning their kit, not a flicker of recognition on their faces, just pure hostility and disdain. As I stood there wondering how best to react, I suddenly became aware that the Corporal was standing behind me conducting the guys as they muttered in unison 'Uneasily, uneasily, uneasily, uneasily!'

It is the only time in my life that I hit an NCO. I grabbed a pillow and set about him, shortly to be joined by my soldiers. The mess of flying feathers was indescribable and cost us dearly when the barrack room was inspected for a 'march out' check the next morning. But I seemed to have passed the test. Over some beers afterwards, my reaction was hailed with approval and helped mould the Troop's incredible comradeship that stuck with us throughout our time in Korea. From then things improved.

I was so very fortunate to have gained my initial experience under the tutelage of these marvellous men. Obviously as I write this book, such experience is no longer available to be passed down but I do commend young officers and NCOs in the 21st century to read the stories of these heroes.

# Chapter 1

# A Journey to Korea

## Liverpool, 27 October 1952

Early one October morning, the Regiment assembled at Ludgershall Halt near Andover. We had thinned out soldiers under the age of 18 and those who had less than eight months still to serve but pulled in tankies from other regiments to bring us up to full strength. We boarded a special train (hauled by the LMS steam engine 'Royal Tank Corps') to Liverpool where we arrived alongside our troop ship berthed on the quay just opposite the famous Liver Birds building.

Once aboard, we lined up along the railings of the starboard deck. Below us on the dockside, faces upturned, were several parents, wives and girlfriends who had come to see us off. Major General N. Duncan, the Representative Colonel Commandant of the RTR and many other officers came to the port to wish all ranks farewell. The Regimental 'Cambrai Band' played rousing tunes, including the Regimental quick march, My Boy Willie, to cheer us as we cast off and headed down the Mersey out to the Irish Sea. As we left, we could hear the band playing a deeply nostalgic rendition of Auld Lang Syne. It was difficult to keep a dry eye.

An hour or so later, before those of us on the officers' deck even had time to organise ourselves in our cabins, dinner was called. As we assembled in the dining room, the ship left the calm waters of the Mersey and entered the Irish Sea. As the ship progressed, the seas grew rougher and rougher. Before long the number of diners diminished and I noticed my cabin mate, Desmond Bastick, scrape his chair back and hurtle for the exit. He was not to reappear at table until we were off Cape St Vincent three days later.

Liverpool, 27 October 1952. We sailed at dusk on HMT *Empire Halladale*. 12 hours out we ran into a heavy gale in the Irish Sea.

Fortunately, I was unaffected and spent a lot of time enjoying the solitude on deck. Somewhere out in the Bay of Biscay, I watched a fair-sized cargo vessel being tossed around like a plastic boat in a child's bath and we heard that all the fishing fleets had fled to port for safety.

Down below, the 400 soldiers in hammocks or bunks in the giant holds, had a horrible time but there was nothing anyone could do. Most were so ill that even words of optimism such as 'the Captain says it will get better tomorrow' failed to produce a reaction. The crew and particularly the chefs aboard, were totally unfazed by a bit of bad weather and continued to cater for every man and woman aboard, even if only a few managed to appear for meals.

The storm's full fury lasted for three really long days before gradually subsiding over the next 24 hours and then, total bliss, we awoke on the fifth morning in calm waters with the majestic Rock of Gibraltar on our port beam. By the time we reached Port Said, we considered ourselves to be seasoned sailors and life on board began to settle into a routine.

*Above and below*: The Bay of Biscay, 29th October 1952. It was the storm of storms. It sent most to their cabins or bunks and kept them there for 2 or 3 days. However all was well by the time we passed Cape St Vincent.

## The *Empire Halladale*

We had joined Her Majesty's Troopship, the *Empire Halladale* in Liverpool. She would carry the Regiment all the way to Pusan in Korea and take about six weeks to complete the journey. Built as the *Antonio Delfino* by Germany's Hamburg South America Line, she had started the 1939 war as a passenger liner off South America. At the outbreak of the war, she had run a Royal Navy blockade off the Brazilian coast and returned to Germany where she served as an accommodation ship for the Kriegsmarine's submarine trainees. Later she made 5 trips as a transporter, each returning to Copenhagen with over 4000 wounded soldiers and refugees from the Russian encircled areas of East Prussia. She was requisitioned by the UK, becoming the troopship *Empire Halladale* until her breakup in 1956.

The *Empire Halladale* was crewed and owned by the Blue Anchor line but commanded by the 7th Tank Transporter Regiment of the Royal Army Service Corps. For two years from 1946, she was in service from Tilbury to Cuxhaven carrying the wives and children of British Army personnel based in Germany. She would then be tasked to ferry troops to Korea and one of these earlier trips had carried conscript Maurice Micklewhite, later known as the actor Michael Caine, and the 1st Battalion the Royal Fusiliers to and from the conflict.

She travelled slowly, on average about 7 knots and we were frustrated to compare our progress with the SS *Chusan*, a luxury P&O ocean liner which left the UK on the same date but still beat us to Hong Kong despite taking a cruise that included a number of more interesting stops.

Whatever the *Halladale*'s original pretensions were, this was far from a luxury cruise. Throughout the voyage, she listed permanently to port and soldiers developed a natural counterbalance onboard that took a few hours to shake off once ashore.

On this six weeks' voyage, there were to be six ports of call, Port Said, Suez, Aden, Colombo, Singapore and Hong Kong. These stops were not for the passengers' benefit; the coal bunkers, freshwater tanks, stores and larders needed refilling on a regular basis and these halts were primarily to resupply and refuel. As non-fare paying passengers,

HMT *Empire Halladale*, our home for 40 days.

we were given little information about the route and were generally only told about the next port of call, so gossip and speculation fuelled conversation and sweepstakes were run among the enlisted soldiers. The mood on board was generally positive, though for some, it took a while to adjust to life at sea. Many were excited to travel, particularly the younger junior ranks, of whom a large number were national servicemen and had not been out of the UK before (some not even to Germany). Most officers above the rank of Lieutenant were seasoned veterans of the desert war and El Alamein and had travelled the first part of this route before.

Travelling by ship to a combat zone was a very different experience to flying into Iraq or Afghanistan nowadays in a few short hours. Our trip took 40 days and every mind harboured an unease about the nature of the war we were heading to. There was certainly more time to dwell on the risks and the even greater inner demon that we might funk under pressure. Our overriding inner fear was that we would be cowardly and let our comrades and the Regiment down under shell fire.

## Life on Board the *Empire Halladale*

To counter the apprehension, the squadron was kept fit, healthy and mentally active. As far as the confined conditions allowed, training continued as if on land and although there were no vehicles on board, there were opportunities to familiarise ourselves with the other equipment we used.

While at sea, we fell into a daily pattern of work and relaxation. Dick Ward saw to it that the soldiers had at least three or four hours training each day after a morning parade so gradually we learned to improve our proficiency with the tools of the trade. We all learned skills such as how to strip, clean and reassemble a machine gun whilst blindfolded, and since we would be working with many national armies, became word perfect in the updated international phonetic military alphabet, using Alpha, Bravo, Charlie etc. instead of the familiar Apple, Baker etc.

Aboard the *Empire Halladale*, I was appointed as Regimental Signals Officer (RSO) and was responsible for ensuring that the signals equipment was operational and the soldiers were proficient in its use. We were moving

We passed through Port Said and took on fresh water but we weren't allowed ashore because of regional tension.

to newer radio systems to replace the wartime era No 38 and No 11 predecessors. Tanks in Korea were operating the Wireless set 88 to speak to nearby supporting units and the more powerful Wireless set No 19 to contact larger formations in depth positions further away. They were still analogue radios but used VHF/FM frequencies and were more reliable. Tuning in the radios on our tanks required a lot more than just pressing a button and we had to acquire the skill of listening to the delicate rise and fall of a central signal and tuning the radio to receive the 'null' in the master signal strength. I ran daily training and familiarisation courses on the new technology and by the time we arrived at the front line, the Regiment was able to use the new systems.

At Liverpool, the soldiers boarded with their issued kit and weapons only, limited to the clothing and equipment they could carry in their kit bags and packs. Arms drills and weapon training continued on board and dress standards were maintained. Generally, discipline was relaxed in some areas, such as in the living areas in the holds, but shaving, hygiene and health precautions were rigorously enforced. Daily parades and roll calls were held and most days included some physical training where the PTIs (physical training instructors) adapted the fitness regime to the conditions and equipment available on board. Inter regimental tug of war matches, deck hockey and boxing between the squadrons became routine events, although ball games, like volleyball, only lasted until the balls were lost overboard.

The days passed swiftly and cheerfully and were rounded off by sing songs on deck in the evening with occasional organised entertainment, rather like prisoner of war camps in the war. It is amazing how much talent lies hidden amongst groups of men and women. We had an accomplished hypnotist with us who put randomly picked soldiers under his spell, getting them to eat raw onions while under the impression they were chomping through juicy apples. On one occasion, unfortunately rather expensively, he persuaded a soldier that his feet were on fire. The poor guy, hopping from foot to foot, pulled off his boots and flung them overboard! The next morning our Quartermaster somehow produced replacement boots like a rabbit out of a hat for the unfortunate soldier. (Army Quartermasters are a remarkable race – how ever do they do it?)

Below decks, the junior ranks ate well. They were served regular fresh meals in the mess hall prepared by the Anchor Lines' own (mostly Asian) cooks.

Once fallen out for the day, many soldiers played cards and board games, relaxed in one of three bars on board, watched films in the cinema or wandered the deck with a beer, looking out to sea.

Travelling on board the *Halladale* with us and hoping to join their husbands in Hong Kong were a number of families of members of our sister regiment, 7 RTR, based in the colony. Loyalty between the RTR regiments was strong and there was little trouble carrying the wives of brother soldiers, although any daughters older than 17 were a pleasant – if untouchable – distraction. However, the contingency of QARANCs (Queen Alexandra's Royal Army Nursing Corps) aboard were fair game for all despite their commanding officer's matronly attempt to keep them out of the Regiment's grasp.

Officers and senior NCOs lived separately with their own messes (or wardrooms) onboard. While the junior ranks were packed into the holds,

As signals instructor, I spent many hours training the Regiment's tank crews and Squadron HQ staff in the use of the new radio systems.

officers shared twin berth cabins and ate together. Once the ship passed Port Said and entered the Indian Ocean, many soldiers chose to sleep on deck which was cooler and less stuffy than the hold, even in winter. To keep cool in the tropical heat, we cut buckets vertically and wedged these upright into the port holes so that they caught the sea breeze and blew it into our cabins. Officers were entitled to bring civilian clothes with them, normally blazer and flannel trousers which were used for trips ashore.

Education was an important part of every soldier's training and the Regiment took pride in assisting in general literacy and building interest in world affairs. The UN's involvement in the conflict in Korea

*Above and opposite*: There was also time for 'soleil' bashing. Enlisted (Right) and commissioned (Left) could only be identified by their head gear.

had started two years before in 1950 and a squadron from 7 RTR had already served in the conflict. 1 RTR had been in Germany since the Second World War and trained to fight a mobile war against the Soviet armies. There was a real need to readjust the Regiment's focus from the use of tanks as an aggressive mobile deterrent to performing a static support role. The positions on the Korean front line had stabilised after the earlier intense movements of the preceding years and the situation appeared stagnant.

For many on board, Korea was a distant, almost irrelevant, war in an unknown part of the world. Part of the education programme onboard was to drive home its relevance to the same Cold War against communism, albeit against a different set of armies. The enemies' equipment would

On board the days quickly passed. Boxing matches were particularly popular, spectators watching from the crows nests!

be similar but the landscape, tactics, languages and even the allied forces we would have to work with would be different. The Chinese and North Korean forces would be using older Soviet equipment that the regiment would be familiar with but their tactics and leadership would pose different threats. As part of a UN (United Nations) force, we would be working with new allies such as the Turkish, Australian, South African, Canadian and New Zealand forces who we had not worked with in Germany. We would also be fighting alongside United States Marines who had acquired an awesome reputation in the Pacific theatre. We would need to adapt our procedures to work with these new friendly forces. All these changes and challenges had to be understood by every member of the Regiment and the six week journey gave barely enough time to prepare for this paradigm shift.

There were also opportunities to distract the soldiers and officers from the conflict they were heading to and focus on the joys of the journey. Dick Ward, as squadron leader, had instructed different officers to brief every member of B squadron on the history of each port before arrival.

I was allocated Hong Kong with the acerbic comment 'So Mr Selway, you will have four weeks to prepare your talk, so it better be good!' Clearly, we had not embarked on a pleasure cruise and I spent hours in the ship's library extracting nuggets of information about the colony from the Encyclopaedia Britannica.

Forgive me for dragging you backwards again but before sailing onward, this is perhaps an appropriate place to tell a few more stories from those early days in Germany. Shortly before we left Germany for the UK, my first Colonel, Col Peter Sturdee, handed over command to Lt Colonel Gerry Hopkinson DSO, MC. Gerry was commissioned into the Royal Tank Corps in 1930 and served in World War II as Commanding Officer of the 44th Royal Tank Regiment and then, briefly, as acting Commander of 4th Armoured Brigade.

Gerry Hopkinson was a physical giant of a man and had had a very successful 'war' being awarded an OBE and an MC. Now he had the unusual and difficult task of commanding a regiment where all four of his squadron leaders had commanded regiments of their own in the war. Each

We organised inter troop and inter Squadron tug of war matches and most days there was some kind of competition held on deck.

knew their task superbly well and it says much of Colonel Gerry's ability as a leader that he could clearly command the respect of those distinguished officers. He had himself commanded a wartime brigade so also understood a diminished postwar command. His voice over the regimental radio network was distinctive and known to each and every soldier. After the Korean War, Col Gerry went on to command the 4th Division in Germany and we met on several occasions when he awarded sporting trophies to teams I ran.

Indeed, on one occasion in a sailing regatta on the Mohne Dam, he used his shotgun to start the race. I was winning but then the wind died and I got becalmed. With a roar 100 yards away from the shore, he yelled 'Paddle the bloody thing!' and followed up by firing his 'starting gun' in my direction. I paddled as though my life depended on it! A memorable and inspiring leader, like so many of the people I grew to admire, he led by example. Perhaps my respect for him was best shown when some 15 years later I asked him, now in retirement, to become a director of one of my companies.

Colonel Peter was perfectly matched to the general mood at this particular time in the tense 'Cold War' that existed. Back in 1949, on my first morning after joining the regiment in Detmold, the adjutant, Captain Cyril Jolly MC, marched me and my three equally new colleagues in to be introduced to the Colonel. 'Quick march, halt, left turn, salute, stand still.' Nervously we awaited our welcome, all unsure of the kind of reception we might receive. The Colonel looked us up and down and after what seemed like an endless pause, he growled to the adjutant, 'Humph Cyril, in my day 2nd Lieutenants were the scum of the earth. Is anything different now?' 'No Sir,' replied Cyril. 'Then I don't need to see them, send them off to their squadrons.' Such was my official welcome to the 1st Tanks.

A couple of years later, I was in charge of an independent unit in the Regiment, called 'The Headquarters Troop', four tanks whose role was to protect the Colonel and his headquarters in battle. But in peace time we could serve on training exercises as 'enemy' against another squadron. On one such occasion, we were to hold a ridge which was to be 'attacked' by C Squadron. It was a perfect defensive position. I lined up my four tanks about 100 yards from each other behind the crest, out of sight of 'the enemy'. At the appropriate moment as C Squadron came into view about half a mile away, my four tanks moved onto the crest, fired 'blank rounds'

Commanding Officer Lt Col Gerry Hopkinson DSO, MC, later Major General Hopkinson, addresses the Regiment in Korea.

at the enemy and then disappeared back down behind the crest before the enemy could return fire. From there, I in my tank and with two of my troop, hidden by the ridge, broke away as swiftly as we could without raising telltale dust, to a flank about half a mile away. Meanwhile the remaining tank popped up and down in the different locations vacated by us three, giving the impression that all 4 tanks were still on the ridge. Then, as the enemy positioned themselves to attack the ridge, the three break away vehicles suddenly appeared on their flank shooting them up. It was an unqualified victory and the enemy squadron leader – a seasoned and highly charismatic war time commander, Peter Massey, was very flattering in his praise.

However, my bubble soon burst. For some reason which I have long forgotten, back in barracks, I was brought before Colonel Peter and given one hell of a rocket. I remember thinking my career was over and such was my mood, I almost decided to skip the Annual Officers' Regimental Ball held a couple of nights later. I was standing by myself feeling very lonely when the Colonel's wife came up to me and asked me what she had done wrong and why wasn't I asking her to dance? I knew the answer of course – total shame – but it appeared she had had a tipoff for once we started dancing, she said conversationally 'You must be very pleased with yourself. Peter was telling me how brilliantly you did on that exercise the other day. He was very proud of you'. It made me burst with pride but more importantly, I saw it as an example of Colonel Peter's wonderful leadership.

As drivers and gunners crawled over their tanks in barracks doing daily maintenance, almost daily stories were told and retold about Colonel Peter Sturdee. He was an eccentric, admired and indeed widely respected leader with a vivid turn of phrase – particularly over the regimental radio net. Woe betide any Squadron or luckless Tank Commander who did not have their tanks marshalled as instructed. 'C for Charlie, what the hell's going on? You're like a gaggle of schoolgirls milling around, lost in a fantasy world of sex and dreams.' (That would be a very modest reprimand by his standards – but this book is no place to repeat his normal expletives).

Except perhaps for the officer being addressed, we all loved it and so did our soldiers who would retell his chastisements word for word. I think that had Colonel Peter told me and my troop to face certain death, I would have done so unhesitatingly. He had the sort of charisma that inspired that level of loyalty.

## Port Said and the Suez Canal

Now, a year or so later when we were in our troopship on route to Korea, he and his wife, Carmen, appeared unannounced coming up the ship's gangway at Port Said. The ship took a huge list to starboard as officers

*Above and below*: After ten days we awoke to find ourselves at anchor off Port Said. We weren't allowed ashore at Port Said, so the locals came out in bum boats to sell us souvenirs while we replenished our fresh water and waited to enter the canal.

*Above and below*: We sailed down the Suez Canal and passed the base at Shamur where we would be based after Korea.

*Above and below*: Colonel Peter Sturdee and his family came aboard and stayed with us down the Suez Canal. We sailed with the evening convoy and were out in the Red Sea when we awoke the next morning.

and sergeants crowded round him. We learned that he had been posted as Military Attaché in Baghdad and had travelled over to Egypt specially to wish us all good luck.

It was this memory of a great leader which stuck in my mind as much as the vibrant and colourful hustle and bustle of our stops at Port Said and Suez with the array of 'bum boats' selling all sorts of produce and its 'Gully Gully' men who came on board pulling live chickens out of their 'Thobes' and other amazing tricks.

This colourful scene was something glamorous that you miss nowadays as you fly swiftly overhead with a laconic announcement by the aircraft Captain: 'We are now flying over the Nile and if you look down quickly, you will just catch a glimpse of the Suez Canal!'

## Aden

There was already tension in Egypt between the locals and the British military presence in the Canal Zone which was the main source of resentment.

*Above and opposite above*: In the Red Sea we passed an American Naval Squadron before arriving at Aden. The approach and berthing caused much interest as for the first time we were to go ashore. We went swimming and sightseeing, then for a swim and drinks at the R.A.F Officers Club.

Consequently, we were kept onboard while the *Empire Halladale* refuelled at Port Said and stayed aboard down the canal until we arrived at the British colony in Aden, now a part of Yemen. It was very hot and when we were finally allowed ashore after ten days on board, the first thing most of us did

We were finally allowed ashore at Aden.

was go for a swim. We spent a day exploring Aden's Souqs full of Oriental nicknacks and later we were hosted at the Officers' Club at the Royal Air Force base before returning to our bunks on the *Empire Halladale*.

*Above, below and opposite above*: We found Aden a frightfully smelly and dirty town – the inhabitants were very idle and slept or lounged all day but the police were surprisingly smart and modern and at least the taxis were efficient.

A typical scene in one of the main streets in Aden.

Despite the attractions on shore, and rumours abounded about the variety of exotic charms availed of, throughout the entire voyage, no officer or soldier in the Regiment was late re-boarding or worse, left behind.

## Colombo and Singapore

The two week voyage to Singapore was filled with more training but I remember a short shore leave in Ceylon, now Sri Lanka, while the *Halladale* took on fuel and fresh water.

Although it rained all day, we walked around the city and took a ride around the seafront. We shopped for a while and managed to go swimming at a local beach and the day ended with dinner at the Galle Face Hotel in Colombo. It was a wonderful cool building with magnificent stairways leading to verandas and terraces overlooking the sea and the city. The bars were very smart and we had a riotous evening unwinding from the encroaching showdown.

Our short visit ashore in Singapore a few days later was similar to Colombo, but with more shops. The highlight of my shore leave in Singapore was a trip to a cinema where I had my first experience of air conditioning … wow, what a difference to life it made that night – and was to make in my future life, large parts of which I spent in the Tropics, particularly around the GCC countries.

*Above, opposite and overleaf*: The entrance to Colombo. Whenever we approached land everyone on board came on deck to watch. Very few of us had been to these places before.

*Right and below*: Singapore was a large, modern and uninteresting city and oppressively warm. We were all glad to get a swim, even though it rained. Apart from the bars on board the *Halladale* there wasn't much to spend our pay on, so we had to make the most of the few hours we had on shore before heading back to the *Halladale*.

Singapore was the scene of a shameful British surrender to the Japanese less than ten years before we arrived and still a fresh sore. Looking at the British defences as we sailed into the harbour we were shocked to see so many original concrete emplacements still standing that had failed to hold the City. The Japanese had simply bypassed the sea defences and walked into the city across the strait from Malaysia. It was a sound warning that war was unpredictable. The Galle Face Hotel in Colombo was reputed to be the oldest hotel east of Suez and it, and the Raffles Hotel in Singapore where we had a drink, were touted as two of the 1000 places to see before you died. As we inched closer to Korea each day we just hoped we'd experience some of the other 998 wonders.

*Above, opposite and overleaf*: Scenes from our visit to Singapore.

## Hong Kong

All our training on board was done under the eagle eye of Dick Ward and needless to say, any weaknesses were quickly exposed and dealt with. Thus, it was with trepidation that I gave my presentation on Hong Kong the day before we arrived there. I had read everything I could find in the ship's library about the colony and prepared a thrilling talk about the colony's history and culture. Most interestingly I thought, I had discovered that its citizens were cremated and their urns kept by the dozen on a shelf in their family's living room. Unfortunately most cultural, historical and industrial references went over my audience's head and frankly I was starting to lose them.

Then came my salvation. I had got onto piracy, the Opium Wars and the War of Jenkins Ear, during which the Chinese had cut off the ear of poor old Mr Jenkins leading to our taking over the colony in retaliation. I then got on to junks and was just describing their importance when I saw behind the soldiers who were sitting in front of an open hatch, a fleet of 20 or 30 sailing

An example of the junk that perfectly illustrated my lecture.

past. Inspired and somewhat relieved at this timely display, I explained that at great expense I had arranged with the British Governor of Hong Kong to send some junks to greet us. If they were to glance out of the hatchway at that moment, they could see some on our port bow.

In the end the talk was well received and in the six or eight weeks of knowing Dick Ward, it was the first time I got a glimmer of praise from him!

Our final stop before Korea was Hong Kong where with heavy hearts, at the officers' dinner on board, we bade farewell to the section of Queen Alexandra nurses who had travelled with us this far. I recall that Capt. Chris

*Above, opposite above and opposite below*: The SS *Chusan*, a luxury P&O liner had left Liverpool at the same time, was docked at Port Said when we passed through, and was already in Kowloon docks. It had also been to Bombay, Colombo and Singapore and still beat us to Hong Kong Island.

9

Snowden had become a centre of attraction with the ladies much to the envy of the more junior subalterns.

That night Lieutenant Tony Uloth performed a song he had written in the Calypso style, 'The 1st Royal Tanks Calypso'. It went...

*The Queen she say to the CIGS,*
*Korea it's in an awful mess.*
*We must have someone*
*to help the Yanks.*
*Of course they chose*
*the First Royal Tanks.*

*Sing, sing, sing with us,*
*The First Royal Tanks Calypso.*
*The Ministry of Transport want a ship,*
*That will make the long, long trip.*
*The only one that was up for sale,*
*Was the* Empire Halladale.

*Sing, sing, sing with us,*
*the First Royal Tanks Calypso.*

It went on for 6 or 8 verses, perhaps someone will remind me of the rest – but as we progressed eastwards, another updated verse was added.

*Temperatures of ninety degrees Fahrenheit,*
*Lord knows what tomorrow night.*

When we anchored in Hong Kong harbour, the officers and men were taken ashore while the ship was being re-victualled. For the 24 hours we were there, we were entertained by the 7th Royal Tank Regiment stationed in Hong Kong. At that time there were 8 regiments in the RTR, down from an astonishing wartime requirement for 40 regiments a few years before. 7 RTR were based on Hong Kong Island and patrolled the New Territories on the Chinese border, in case China made a play for the Colony. C Squadron of 7 RTR was the first British armoured unit to go to Korea and had fought a manoeuvre war in Churchill Mk VII tanks equipped with flame throwers. They had lost four soldiers. Despite 7 RTR's proximity to Korea, being fully acclimatised to the Asian climate and familiar with the terrain, the Ministry of Defence was reluctant to send the Hong Kong garrison again since the threat level from the Chinese was heightened. 1RTR would sail on to Korea instead with its expertise on the more modern Centurion tanks but 7 RTR's experience and advice those nights would prove invaluable.

The 7th were (mostly) grateful to be safely reunited with their wives and children who had travelled out on the *Halladale* with us and in return for their deliverance we enjoyed the most amazing, unexpected hospitality. It was one of those marvellous examples of military comradeship which makes soldiering so rewarding.

We were wined and dined so royally that my memories of those hours ashore are exceedingly dim but luckily I have several photos to remind me

*Above and overleaf*: We had a splendid day, swimming, eating, drinking and shopping.

of that visit. Of course, the hospitality didn't just extend to the officers. Few of my soldiers remember getting back on board after similar treatment by their opposite numbers in the 7th but by a miracle, not one soldier was left behind! What I do remember, as the ship got underway for Pusan in South Korea, was the flotilla of small boats crewed by waving members of the 7th escorting us out of the harbour.

In Hong Kong, our Squadron 2 i/c (second in command), Arthur Thrift MC, rejoined us. He had been sent ahead to Korea by air as our 'advance party' to learn from the Skins who we were replacing, about the role we were to perform. Over the next four days or so before we reached Pusan, he briefed us on what to expect when we landed. The reality of our imminent arrival

The 7th Tanks were our hosts for two days and turned out in strength in small boats to see us off on the last stage of our journey.

at the 'sharp end' and the heads up about our role once on the ground added a real sense of urgency to our last chances to prepare. As reality hit hard, training on board the *Halladale* took on a sinister urgency and intensity.

It never ceases to amaze me how your sea legs grow. As we buffeted our way north towards our final destination, we encountered the edge of a typhoon but on this occasion, I cannot recall one person missing a meal including the delicious farewell dinner.

In passing it was all too common to criticise the good ship *Halladale* with its permanent list to port, so much so that those onboard experienced some difficulty walking upright when they first went ashore. When we raised our concerns, it was explained that if the ship was upright at sea, the pipes in the Ship's Engineer's cabin gurgled so loudly, they kept the poor man awake. It was therefore understood by the crew that under no circumstances were they to empty the port bilges. The crew looked after us astonishingly well and sadly I don't think in the excitement of the moment they were ever properly thanked.

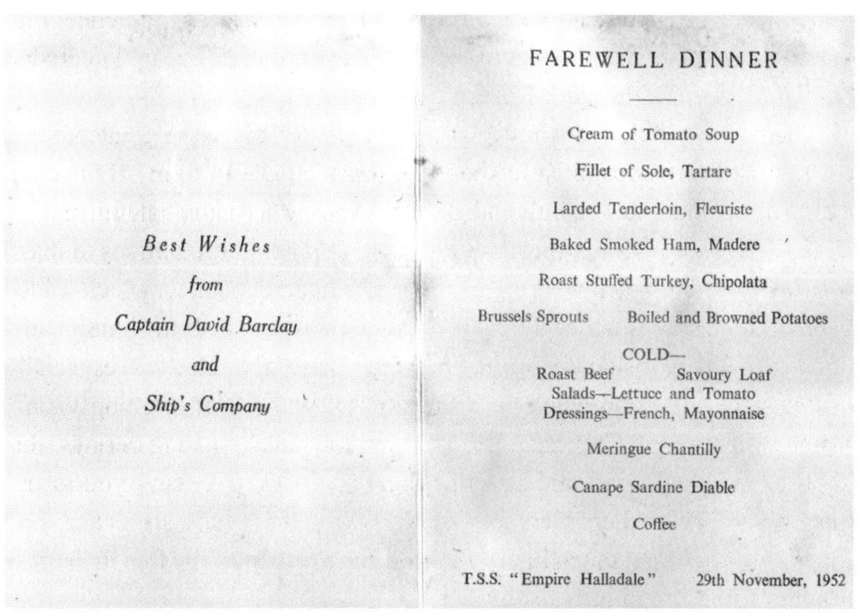

*Best Wishes*
*from*
*Captain David Barclay*
*and*
*Ship's Company*

FAREWELL DINNER

Cream of Tomato Soup

Fillet of Sole, Tartare

Larded Tenderloin, Fleuriste

Baked Smoked Ham, Madere

Roast Stuffed Turkey, Chipolata

Brussels Sprouts Boiled and Browned Potatoes

COLD—
Roast Beef Savoury Loaf
Salads—Lettuce and Tomato
Dressings—French, Mayonnaise

Meringue Chantilly

Canape Sardine Diable

Coffee

T.S.S. "Empire Halladale" 29th November, 1952

Printed menu from the Farewell dinner, 29th November 1952. The Anchor Line looked after us magnificently.

# Chapter 2

# Frozen Frontlines

## Our Arrival in Korea

As we sailed into Pusan harbour, the ship's rails were crowded as everyone came up to the decks to catch a first glimpse of Korea. From the ship the view of the bleak and barren Korean hills was uninspiring. There were one or two naval vessels escorting the ships coming into Pusan but there were no obvious signs yet that we were entering a war zone or that troop ships were endangered.

Before we disembarked, a supply of clothing was brought on board and issued to help us contend with the Korean Winter. We had travelled with our issued uniforms and tank coveralls, adequate for European winters but barely effective in the stark Korean conditions.

The new kit included warm 'Parka' jackets to replace the greatcoat that the first British troops in Korea had found inadequate to fight off the cold. This pattern of parka was influenced by the American Army 'Fishtail' parkas already in use by US marines in Korea, and featured large buttons to make it easier to fasten when wearing gloves and extended pockets which folded back on themselves under the flap. It also featured a thick fur lining and a hood with a wire inside the brim to help keep its shape. This was especially useful since the hood acted as a face guard, without obstructing vision. When watching the Chinese positions from the tanks for long periods, this kept the freezing wind and rain off your face while allowing you to use binoculars. The soldiers were also issued with gloves, hats, socks and long johns, which caused much hilarity at the time because of the flap in the rear but they too came in jolly useful.

Soldiers also received many items from home by post, often from strangers. I wrote a letter to the *Hendon Times* to thank its local community for sending out homemade knitwear. These gifts were popular and gratefully

The official reception to Korea was a well-oiled stage-managed production that happened on a weekly basis. Pusan, 6 December 1952. Bands, (Jazz and conventional) met us together with a routine reception committee – Colonel Gerry received a large bouquet.

received by the men who struggled to stay warm, especially while 'standing to' in their tanks for two hours every dawn and dusk. They acted as an important reminder that home hadn't forgotten us despite there being half a world between us, and their support was invaluable to our morale.

Certainly warmer winter clothing had been desperately needed but once the men were kitted out I rarely heard of a soldier succumbing to the weather despite the bitter winter conditions.

*Above and overleaf*: Queuing to draw winter clothing. This was excellent kit and would come in useful as we set off for the bitter overnight journey in an archaic, wooden-seated, unlit and window-paneless train to the front. The tank crews were prioritised since they had to leave immediately for the front or miss the handover from the Skins who were leaving the next day. The remainder were kept aboard the *Halladale* in Pusan for two days to draw kit and prepare.

We found that temperatures caused the ground to freeze solid for 6 feet or more and sitting stationary in the tanks on watch for eight hour shifts during the winter was a challenging and numbing experience. The temperature range and weather conditions in Korea over our tour were extreme; during the summer, rations could be cooked on the tank's metal decks but it also rained, especially in the monsoon season, and the rain made watching from open hatches a miserable experience. With no need to watch for air attack, we were grateful to the Squadron's fitters who fashioned rain covers for us.

Headgear was also a contentious issue. Inside tanks, steel helmets, which were enforced across most of the front line, were a curse; they were large and hindered mobility in vehicles and there was also no need for more metallic protection, the 50 tonnes of steel were quite sufficient. The Royal Tank Corps had pioneered the beret as the perfect headgear when

We arrived in the harsh Korean December. Luckily the issued Winter clothing was excellent. The parka coats over our tank coveralls were especially welcome. The extremes in temperature in Korea would challenge the QM stores in different ways. From extreme cold in winter...

buttoned up inside a tank. It had been adapted from the headgear of French Alpine soldiers in 1917 by Generals Elles and Beresford for tank crewmen. They provided some protection from sharp metal edges inside the tank, were light, looked smart and the radio's headphones fitted comfortably over them. Unlike other Armoured Regiments, the Royal Tank Regiment had adopted the black beret as its only official headgear and it became a

...to intense summer heat. Not even our Quarter Master could source non-melting candles for the officers' mess!

signature and highly identifiable piece of uniform that the soldiers took great pride in wearing. Even Field Marshall Montgomery had shed his infantry origins and adopted the RTR beret (not his mother regiment) for his iconic wartime image. A compromise was reached; berets onboard and helmets only if required.

Arriving alongside the dock in Pusan, we were greeted by Colonel Gerry Hopkinson, who had flown on ahead from Hong Kong and a Korean reception committee that included a small and brightly attired young girl in traditional clothing. She presented Colonel Gerry with a huge bouquet while a large American Marine band provided rousing music. This band not only played some conventional 'military' tunes but played a popular song 'If I knew you were coming, I'd have baked a cake'. It later broke into some jazzy numbers as it marched and 'pirouetted' up and down the quayside. This was a well rehearsed and oft-performed programme every troopship arriving at Pusan had remarked on and I'm afraid I recall looking pompously down my nose at this rather effete exhibition and thinking it was 'not quite the thing for a military band'!

*Above left and above right*: Disembarking in Pusan. The enlisted soldiers were initially limited to the clothing and items they could carry.

On arrival in Pusan and ashore after all those weeks at sea Trooper Delaney looks apprehensive whilst Corporal Pearson calls the Roll! The tank crews disembarked first to rush up to the line to take over from the Skins.

B Sqn Officers ashore in Pusan before boarding the train to the front lines; (L-R) Micky Farmer, the Author, Dick Ward, Chris Snowden, Martin Sinnett and Mike Colston. (Less Vic Senior and Arthur Thrift). We are carrying sticks called 'ash plants'. In the very boggy battlefields of Flanders in 1916, officers frequently preceded their tanks in battle on foot, prodding the ground with sticks to check for solid ground. In their memory, RTR officers still carry 'ash plants'.

## Impressions of Korea

From the pre-war 40-year-old *Empire Halladale*, we embarked on what was probably an even older steam train to take us for the 12 to 14 hour journey to Tokchon, a small station an hour and a half by truck from the frontlines.

I doubt the train went over 20 mph and some of the windows were void of glass, generating a bitter cold draught! At the start of our journey, as we wended our way slowly through Pusan, we had our first sights of the Korean interior. We saw hundreds of displaced citizens, the lucky ones living in homes made from 'shipping containers' and the less lucky ones living in large cardboard boxes bound together. Running alongside the slow moving train were seriously undernourished and near naked children begging for sweets and money. It painted a grim picture of a battered nation.

The appalling squalor of the city – about 10 people lived in each of these shacks by Pusan Station.

Throughout the tour of Korea, there were opportunities to mix with Korean nationals. Many Korean peasants lived and continued to farm around the rear areas and close to the front lines, although the area of no man's land between the North Korean/Chinese and UN front lines was abandoned, and the paddy fields there understandably untended. They were mostly very poor farmers and because most didn't seem to own beasts of burden, carts, or vehicles, were nearly always bowed down with heavy loads on their backs supported by a wooden 'A' frame piled high with wood or straw.

While we were in reserve, contact with Korean civilians was mostly limited to children begging sweets, money or clothing, or farmers selling produce to supplement our rations. Many thousands of Korean men acted as porters for the UN forces, working for the KSC (Korean Service Corps) and helping with logistical support and defensive construction, often in danger and under fire. Unfortunately, they wore clothes (padded jackets and cloth caps) that were very similar to the Chinese forces, often causing confusion since they were frequently mistaken for assaulting troops. Many others were killed by Chinese fire while performing these services. For the enlisted men, an opportunity to trade government property for favours from young Korean ladies had to be clamped down on as girls were often apprehended leaving the rear areas with multiple layers of towels, socks and shirts hidden under their dresses.

*Above and below*: The countryside wasn't much better. The villages were poor, simple and lacked any 20th century technology. The fields were fertilised with human sewage and stank. We felt we had travelled back to the Dark Ages.

I found the Korean people were largely supportive of the United Nations' efforts and bitter towards the Chinese. We did not consider the locals as hostile or suspect them of spying; certainly not in the way that locals were mistrusted and alienated in later wars such as Vietnam.

This faith in the locals' support might not have been entirely justified; somehow the Chinese forces heard of our arrival and when we took our positions on the line, we heard the PVA welcome B Squadron the Royal Tank Regiment to the front line over the loud speaker system they set up to broadcast propaganda. I'm fairly sure I heard messages directed at me personally to go home in case I was killed. I can only think they had

Many Koreans lived simply, in small houses surrounded by paddy fields.

As soon as we left Pusan, the squalor and poverty of the countryside became apparent.

local sources for this level of detail. The lack of education or political participation among the Korean peasants was remarkable and contrasted with the degree of anger in the towns about any appeasement in the terms of the proposed truce and the UN's failure to enforce a complete unification of South Korea with the North. These images are etched on my memory and are in incredible contrast to modern Korea.

Indeed, what an amazing 60 year story of national recovery followed.

Modern timber buildings in Pusan belied the scenes we could expect up-country.

Most of the population in the Korean countryside lived in small huts that were more rudimentary than we had seen anywhere.

Tokchon-apart from the railway station, the place was very poor.

It has shown human resourcefulness at its very best and, in my mind, served more than anything else to justify the stand the United Nations took in deciding to defend Southern Korea against Communism in 1950! Not only Korea but the world is a better place because of this courageous decision.

An all too familiar sight, a peasant struggling under a load of firewood.

Korean porters could be identified by the 'A' frame back packs with which they carried considerable loads. Many worked and died supplying the UN frontlines, either through indirect Chinese artillery fire or from stepping on mines left behind when the PVA had withdrawn through the area earlier in the war.

Reverting to the journey, the next morning, having suffered a pretty sleepless uncomfortable journey, we arrived at the railhead behind the frontlines and were given an enthusiastic reception by some members of the 5th Royal Inniskilling Dragoon Guards (the 'Skins') who were heading to

Pusan and then homewards on the *Halladale*. They had been in Korea since the preceding December and been heavily engaged during the second battle of the Hook only a few days before and were happy their tour had ended. Their lorries drove us from the train station directly to the tank positions on the front line where we arrived just before nightfall to meet the last Skins on the line.

*Above*: This family ran a shop by the station.

*Right*: Poverty was everywhere you looked in the countryside. A farmer carries a typical 'A' frame load beside a cart along the main supply route.

In Seoul, the Koreans were not as keen as we were in arranging an armistice – I don't think these schoolgirls realised they were distributing pamphlets calling for 'Unification or Death!'.

At regular convoy resting points, the Koreans quickly set up roadside shops selling souvenirs.

*Above and overleaf*: In Seoul, the townsfolk were more prosperous and educated. Many government buildings had a European/American classical design which reflected their aspirations although there was still evidence of a classical Asian world, such as the Western Gate.

NAME
PLATE
NO.1 STORE

Seoul Market Place. Seoul was an hour by jeep from the reserve positions and we could go in when we didn't have any duties. We spent hours wandering around the markets and shops.

*Previous page bottom, above and left*: Generic scenes of daily life in South Korea. Whilst in reserve we were able to travel and meet the locals. In town and the countryside, we moved freely and the people were cheerful and genuinely welcoming.

There was a lack of technology in the countryside and each family member was expected to lend a hand.

## Handover at the Front

The RTR would form the armoured backbone of the 1st Commonwealth Division which held its sector of the front with its three Brigades in the line, each Brigade having a battalion in reserve. On the left was 25 Canadian Infantry Brigade with 'B' Squadron Lord Strathcona's Horse in support (who were placed under operational control of the Regiment). The central sector was held by 29 British Infantry Brigade, with 'B' Squadron commanded by Major Ward in support and the right sector by 28 Britcom (British and Commonwealth) Infantry Brigade with 'A' Squadron commanded by Major Howard Jones in support. 'C' Squadron commanded by Major Maunsell went into Divisional reserve, South of the River Imjin.

As we were shown the positions we would take over from the Skins, we had an opportunity to look through the Centurion's powerful x10 tank periscope binoculars and observe the Chinese frontline positions for the first time. They were about a mile away, at about our height, on the hillside across a flat-bottomed valley several hundred feet below us. Ready or not, we had arrived at the war.

A typical picture of the 'front line' overlooking Chinese positions across the valley. The troop leader's position overlooking the feature 'Churchill'.

3 Troop, fresh on the line at Point 187, Corporal Goldie with Troopers Couzens, McLean, Howarth and above, Stradling.

At that stage of the war, the Commonwealth division predominantly faced Chinese forces from the 65th and 63rd Armies of the People's Volunteer Army (PVA).

By the late autumn of 1952 the Chinese defences stretched back for some twenty miles and it was estimated that they had 900 pieces of artillery and seven Chinese armies totalling 160,000 men facing the UN armies. Many Chinese soldiers had been trained by the US to fight the Japanese in WW2 and knew our tactics.

It is hard to imagine a smoother and more successful handover under active service conditions than the Skins accorded to us all. As I recall,

(From left to right). The author, with Troopers Devine, Rushman and Kirk. It was as cold as it looks.

we arrived in the evening and were quickly shown the positions of their '3 Troop B squadron'. All armoured regiments were formed up with the same number of squadrons and troops with the same subunit designations, so it was easy to 'mirror' and slot into another armoured regiment's positions.

The North Korean Army was weak, poorly trained and under equipped, even by Chinese standards, and rarely used for front line work in our sector. The Chinese armies lacked airpower of any description but had strong and capable artillery forces and possibly a few tanks, operating (like ours at this stage of the war) in fire support roles. Their infantry attacks were typically preceded by massive artillery bombardments and carried out in human waves on foot, with great courage and at great cost to themselves. These were preceded by distinctive bugle calls and then the approaches to our positions were swarmed with thousands of attacking PVA infantry, some

Taking stock of my new situation! Sitting behind the firing position, with the empty cases from the previous night's fire support. For tank crews, issued hob nailed boots were often replaced by warmer, drier and more practical footwear, in this case German Army jackboots.

armed only with grenades. While the truce talks were underway, the UN forces were unlikely to advance themselves but the Chinese still fielded a force of over 1.3 million expendable soldiers and were determined to emerge from the war with, at the very least, a propaganda success. Our job was to prepare and hold off these attacks. Always present in the back of our minds were the experiences of the Gloucester Regiment the year before which occurred less than five miles away from where we now stood.

The Skins explained to us that after dusk, infantry from both sides sent standing patrols down to the bottom of the valley ready to give early warning of any night attack by the enemy. Sometimes these standing patrols turned into aggressive fighting patrols designed to dominate no man's land. At such times we would be called on to give fire support.

We were also introduced to the local infantry battalion, which at that time was a Scottish regiment, the Black Watch. Our troop command posts (CPs) were always sited with the infantry's who were dug in on the reverse slopes just behind our positions. It was explained that I would spend a lot of time with the local infantry commanding officer so had better get on with them. This tank troop to infantry battalion relationship gave a huge career advantage to tank regiment officers because a tank troop subaltern was embedded with and dealt directly with the battalion's commanding officer, normally a Lt Colonel. This exposure to the vast experience of a senior officer gave junior tank commanders unrivalled insight into command at a senior level and helps account for the disproportionate ratio of armoured officers on the general staff.

After that briefing, I and my tank commanders gathered in the troop commander's hoochies (the infantry called them hutchies), with maps spread out for a further briefing. We were also shown the settings for our guns to fire at pre-arranged targets. Afterwards, the troops from both armoured regiments that were not on watch got together in the dead ground behind the tanks and a campfire was lit, beers and food were circulated and before long a singsong started. What I remember most of that night was the Skins singing their own version of 'We are Moving on'.

*'We are saying goodbye to the rest of you guys,*
*because we are moving on*
*it won't be long and then we are gone,*
*cos we are moving on'.*

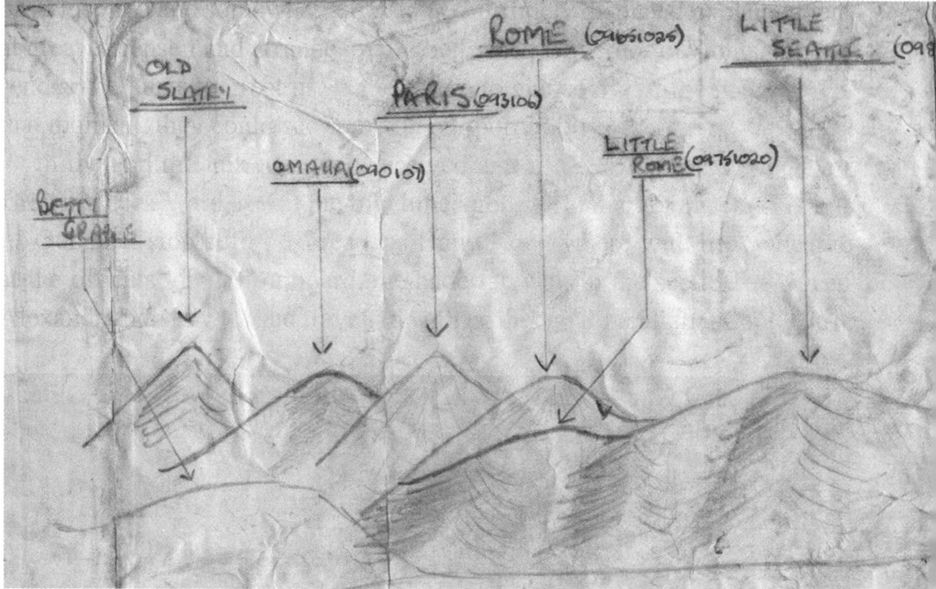


At every position we drew a panoramic sketch of the main geographic landmarks to quickly identify features, in the event of needing to rapidly report enemy activity. This is my panorama / range card from my tank's position on 187 overlooking the Chinese positions across the valley on the opposing hillside.

I wish I could remember the rest of the verses. It was a happy, morale building sendoff as we knew we were taking over tanks which were well sited, well designed and in top condition. We had been well briefed and were confident we knew what was expected of us.

The next morning the Skins had gone and my troop was left alone on a hilltop feature, known by its altitude above sea level as 'Point 159'. On three sides of this position, the PVA looked down on the defences and fired so continuously that there was no vegetation left on the hill. Behind this position to the East was the highest UN-held feature called Little Gibraltar.

I began my first day by getting to know the local infantry company commanders; majors from the Black Watch included Majors Claude Moir, Angus Irwin and Tony Lithgow and their CO Lieutenant Colonel David Rose. The Black Watch had been heavily engaged in the 2nd Battle of the Hook (18/19 November 1952) less than a fortnight before we arrived in Korea and some of their positions were overrun by the PVA.

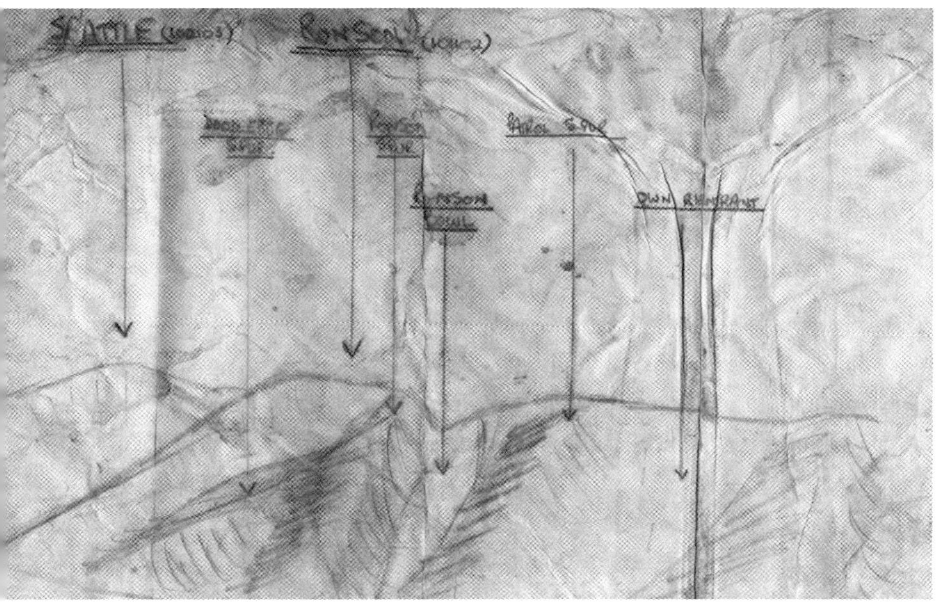

The Black Watch had taken casualties, around 20 killed and around 50 wounded and eleven of their soldiers had been captured. In the process of recapturing the position, a Centurion of the Skins had been knocked out. If further proof that I was in the middle of something deeply serious was needed, speaking with the Black Watch major about his experiences on this spot just a few weeks before confirmed the reality of the situation and the danger of underestimating our enemy.

Chinese infantry might not be well equipped but they attacked with massive levels of artillery support and were tenacious. Since the Black Watch had been saved and the lost ground recaptured, thanks largely to a rapid counterattack by a single Centurion from the Skins, the commanding officer fully appreciated the value of tank support. His frank account of the battle helped me understand my role more clearly which in turn helped us work together and I felt immediately that I was a key part of their team.

Throughout their tour in Korea, the 1st Tanks never fought as a complete regiment, with Squadrons united in a dazzling show of manoeuvre and spear-thrusting force. Instead, the squadrons were dispersed into static defensive fighting positions along the front of the Commonwealth Division, which

'We' were on the hills to the left – the Chinese on the hills to the right. The tanks had to be located far enough forward on the hills to be able to fire down into the valleys. Thus, they were clearly visible to the Chinese so protection from incoming fire and screening from view was erected round them so that at least crew changes could largely be concealed.

The author standing behind a Centurion at Point 187. It is entrenched or 'hull down', so that the most vulnerable parts of the tank are protected by earth works.

itself was sandwiched between a US Marine and a South Korean Army (ROK) Division. Even within the squadrons, the troops were detached and independent, working more directly with the infantry units they supported rather than each other. The tanks on the line seldom moved. When we arrived, they were already well sited to provide fire support and overwatch across no man's land and the Chinese positions.

Typically, of the Regiment's three sabre squadrons (each of three troops), two squadrons would be on the line and one held in reserve. A troop might rotate to a different Point each time it rejoined the line and the crews 'hot bed' into different tanks which stayed in position. At each rotation a troop might work with different infantry units within the Commonwealth Division. Tank crews on the front line lived, ate and slept in 'hutchies' close to their tanks and after stand to at first and last light two members of each four man crew were awake and on watch within each tank.

C Squadron supported a Turkish unit. Unfortunately the Turks provided the rations which our own crews found inedible, so the troop in support brought up an Army Catering Corps chef to live on the front line and feed them (much to his displeasure). (Photo by D. Croft)

What a gun!! In reality this was an artillery bombardment, but I couldn't resist the image.

## Squadron Headquarters

The squadron leadership operated from the squadron headquarters a mile or two behind the frontline units, close to the reserve squadron positions, both typically just out of artillery range of the Chinese. This location was across the Imjin River and close to Gloucester Hill, the site of the Gloucester Regiment's last stand the year before. Here you could find the squadron offices, stores, the LAD (Light Aid Detachment) fitters and MT (Motor Transport) sections and the 'bashas' or the troops' and officers' accommodation. Sqn HQ would be in touch via radio or field telephone with the troop CPs and the Brigade and kept informed of any developments at the front. Because the war and front lines had settled to a certain extent, the bashas and SHQ offices had had time to develop into comfortable and semi-permanent structures although tents were sometimes more habitable than Korean farm buildings. Some SHQ personnel, such as the Squadron leader, and members of the LAD Section, lived and worked from caravans.

*Above and below*: The Squadron Headquarters handled all the administration to keep the active troops on the line. It additionally had its own defensive troop of Centurions and a troop in reserve.

The Regiment's Reserve Area across the Imjin River and close to Gloucester Valley.

*Above, opposite above, opposite below and overleaf*: The SHQ office, the officers' lines, A troop 'Basha' and the MT office. The entrance to the Sqn area, the SHQ and the Sqn LAD section workshop (a caravan).

*Right and below*: Michael Colston inspects the perimeter around and approaches to Squadron HQ. This featured lengths of concertina wire and even strategically placed urinals.

## The Centurion Mk III

Of course, the majority of training, logistical support and energy of the Squadron HQ was focussed on delivering fully manned and operational Centurions to the front line where they could make a difference.

The Centurion's main armament was a powerful 20 pounder (84 mm) which fired a variety of rounds, such as high explosive or armour piercing. Its ability to fire directly from its sited positions into the valley made it a formidable deterrent against Chinese advances and also meant that supporting fire for infantry could be delivered more quickly and effectively than artillery. Its uncanny ability to hit a sq. yard target at 1000 yards within 30 seconds of being called on gave the infantry massive confidence in tank support generally. It also fielded a .30 calibre Besa machine gun which was mounted coaxially with the main gun and used the same sights, also controlled by the gunner. This could be a preferred weapon for targets such as infantry moving in the open.

The front of a Mk 3 Centurion main battle tank. One of the most successful postwar tank designs, remaining in production into the 1960s. In action until the 70s and as a combat engineer chassis until the 90s.

When used at night with a searchlight mounted on the tank, (nicknamed a 'Tulip') it could debilitate its target like a rabbit in the headlights. However, searchlights had two drawbacks; first the engines had to be running at almost full throttle to generate sufficient electrical energy to power them and the 'Tulips' attracted enemy fire and were put out of action by Chinese shell fire. The infantry were equipped with some night vision which was effective for controlling our fire onto registered targets and denied the Chinese the night time advantage of ambient light. In fact I don't recall ever using my troop's Tulip.

The Mark III Centurion could only store 62 rounds for the main gun and 4000 rounds for the Besa inside the turret, so extra ammunition (one Squadron fired 504 shells and 22,500 Besa rounds in one night) was stored immediately behind the tank since restocking under bombardment was unpleasant.

Chinese assault troops frequently got very close to our tanks across all sections of the front. On these occasions the 2 inch (51mm) mortar, (known

Australian troops from 2 RAR helping attach the searchlight ('Tulip') to the turret, to line up with the main gun and coaxial Besa machine gun. These were a mixed blessing. Smoke from our own weapons often bounced the light back in our faces so we couldn't see anything while we were firing the Besa machine gun. They also attracted Chinese counter-fire.

My tank – named 'Mersa Mutruh' (after the North African tank battle) positioned on the Hook. 3 Troop, B Squadron commander's personal tank was always called this.

as 'Bomb Throwers') mounted on the turret but fired and loaded from inside, were used to repel them.

The Centurion was particularly appreciated by its crews for the ability of its armour (8 inches in the thickest places) to shrug off Chinese weapons. In the regiment's first month on the line, Lt Duff's Centurion was hit by 5 heavy mortars in a night action and survived. During the 3rd Battle of the Hook, C Squadron's tanks survived an average of at least five hits each from shells and mortars despite all the mounted searchlights being destroyed and deep gashes in the plates.

On the same night, another tank from B Squadron received a direct hit from an 85 mm armour piercing round which made a deep gouge on the nose plate but failed to penetrate the vehicle. Other tanks claimed to have shrugged off 105 mm Chinese anti tank rounds.

The faith in the protection offered by the Centurion meant that tank crews often dashed from the comparative protection of the hutchies in the ground when they came under Chinese artillery fire, preferring the cover provided by their vehicles. Conversely, the infantry took the opposite

Mersa Mutruh and Umbrella! In addition to maintaining the serviceability of the tanks, the LAD section had the tools to make our lives more comfortable and it was well worth keeping the fitters on side. Here the LAD fitted her out with a frame for a tarpaulin top cover to carry us through the rainy season.

Direct mortar impacts on a Centurion at the Hook caused some damage to the storage bins and required a field repair by the fitters to free the turret. In this incident, the crew were barely aware they had been hit. (Photo by Denis Croft)

view and headed for their hutchies. The American forces expressed great admiration for the Centurion but we had considerable sympathy and tried not to dwell on the dangers faced by our neighbouring Canadian armoured regiment, Lord Strathcona's Horse, which was equipped with Sherman tanks. These could be split open by Chinese shells.

In addition to working closely with Commonwealth infantry, as a part of a United Nations force we were deployed next to the US division and our tanks often responded to their fire missions.

It wasn't only the RTR's Centurions that were closely watched by the Americans on the line, one of our officers achieved enduring cultural status! Lieutenant Peter Berry was a very laidback and effective troop leader. An offer had come for a volunteer to be seconded to the American Air Force 'Artillery Spotter squadron'. Their job was the very dangerous one of flying low over the frontlines directing artillery fire. Peter turned out not only to be steely cool and calm in this task but remarkably efficient. The Americans admired his casual British relaxed attitude, plummy

Detail of the Impact damage from a direct hit from a Chinese mortar.

Farewell to 03ZR22 and completing the initial inspection of the new 'Mersa Mutruh'. Handover was a serious business as you signed for responsibility of the new vehicle or issued equipment. Any damage or deficiencies not discovered at this stage could be attributable to you personally. Considerable care was taken not to be faced with a bill for a deficient Centurion! I was still paying for the damage following the pillow fight with my troop before we left for Korea!

Peter Berry went on to be the subject of a regular comic strip in the US Forces paper *Stars and Stripes*.

accent and vivid turn of phrase, so much so that they made him the hero of a daily strip cartoon series in the American Forces daily newspaper, *The Stars and Stripes*. On one occasion, a true story this time, he was depicted viewing his aircraft on return from a mission. It was peppered with bullet holes and the caption underneath was 'Hmm, mice again'. The Yanks loved him.

## The LAD workshop

Each squadron had an LAD (Light Aid Detachment) section from the newly formed Royal Electrical and Mechanical Engineers (REME). These were the fitters and mechanics responsible for maintaining the squadron's vehicles and all of its electrical and mechanical equipment. They were based in the squadron headquarters and would respond to defects, improvements and damage to the vehicles that the crews couldn't fix themselves. Many

The chief fitter, WO1 'Snags' Stacey ran our LAD which worked tirelessly to ensure damaged or faulty tanks were quickly returned to action, often in the front line. A'snag' was a fault or deficiency in an inventory.

If the troop couldn't pull it out, REME would bring in Brigade assets to recover it. In this instance a 'C' Squadron crew managed to embarrass themselves showing off to the infantry. The crew was roundly mocked and possibly sent to submarine school!

of the maintenance and servicing tasks were carried out by the crew such as continually tightening the tracks with a giant ring spanner, cleaning the main gun with a ramrod, changing the oil and some minor common repairs like a thrown track (known as callsign 'Banjo' over the net). For anything else, the LAD performed heroic feats, often in great danger. Anything that the squadron LAD couldn't fix would be sent up the line to the brigade workshops which also held the bulk of the recovery vehicles and lifting equipment.

## 3 Troop, B Squadron

After acting as temporary signals officer on the troopship out to Korea, I resumed command of 3rd troop in 'B' Squadron. Each of the four tanks in the troop had a crew of four, the tank commander, a driver, a gunner and a loader. I was both the troop and a tank commander and my troop sergeant also commanded a tank, as did two senior corporals.

When the tank was running, conversation was difficult and we talked to each other through mics and headsets over a closed telephone system. The Centurion had very advanced radio systems to communicate over different channels (or nets) with either local units or, on another wireless set, with regimental, brigade, or even divisional command. In this close environment where we would spend hours together, I always felt we developed a much closer bond between officers and men than, for instance, the infantry. Remaining aloof or distant simply wasn't workable. The tightest bonds within the Squadrons were between the four crewmen of individual tanks since they worked more closely together than others. This close relationship was also extended from the tank crews to their troop leaders, normally subalterns but sometimes senior sergeants, who commanded both the tank and the troop. These relationships also extended to the commanders and crews of the other tanks in your troop but particularly with your troop

3 Troop, B Squadron, 1 RTR. Pausing after a river crossing to allow support elements to catch up on the return to the reserve area.

sergeant. As mentioned before, no troop job was too degrading for an officer to do, indeed the menial jobs often garnered the most respect.

Troop leaders might well be accountable to their squadron and regiment, but their loyalty was often torn and always the subject of introspection, a subject that filled endless numbers of leadership manuals and still dominates debate around leadership gurus at staff colleges around the world. However, it made the relationship between an armoured troop officer and his men unique in the army.

Many other ranks contributed to the astonishing teamwork found within the 1st Tanks and Shakespeare could not have put it more effectively. We were, as I will attempt to show, a happy band of brothers. For sure, during the year some officers 'got posted', Sergeants were demoted to Trooper

Crossing the Imjin.

and soldiers got into hot water but surprisingly there was no malice, just comradeship. We had a job to do and we all did our best.

The driver of my tank – Michael Devine, known as 'Andy' (so as not to confuse him with the American character actor) – remains one of those tough, resourceful and highly competent Geordies I was lucky enough to serve with. He drove my tank into positions that no other tank could reach. Always cheerful, Andy had a unique way of describing and overcoming challenges. He would attribute names to key components, the clutch shaft became the *fukker,* the gear the *sod* and a main bearing, the *tit*. So when he said 'the *tit* wouldn't engage with the *sod* as the *fukker* had disintegrated' it was always crystal clear to us what he meant and what had to be done.

Later, as we prepared in the dark for yet another Chinese attempt to capture the Hook feature, we were detailed to provide support fire for the local infantry battalion to help prevent them from being overrun by swarms of Chinese soldiers. This task required us to be placed in a prominent

Andy Devine somehow manoeuvred my Centurion several hundred feet higher than the rest of the troop were able to (look closely to see the next nearest below!). That well known lager advertisement had not yet hit the billboards but 'Mersa Mutruh' reached the parts other tanks cannot reach.

position and as commanders we had to sit high up in our tank turrets. Thus, I was conscious that in the dark, a Chinese patrol could well creep up on us and put us out of action. I asked Andy from his driver's position below mine, to keep a careful watch. His reply in his strong Geordie accent is known by every member of my family 'Don't worry Sir, I'll sit here on the wing with my Sten gun and no bloody *fooker* will get us!' Whilst the Hook was being so gallantly defended, no Chinese troops broke through – and I could not have felt safer.

Sergeant Pat Coveney, as my Troop Sergeant, was second in command of the troop and my replacement if things went south. He commanded one

Sgt Coveney outside the crew Hutchie on Point 210. Unlike most Tankies, Pat preferred and was well known for, keeping his 'tin lid' on.

of the troop's tanks and managed the logistical aspects of running the troop, ensuring we were kept supplied and in good order. Thus, after he left the Army, he found his training had prepared him well to run the Blue Posts pub, a well known watering hole, next to the Ritz in Mayfair.

John Nolan was a trooper in B squadron. He later emigrated to Australia and served with the SAS there. He won praise at the fourth Hook battle where his quick cool thinking had saved two of his crew members, wounded when a UN artillery close fire mission damaged his Centurion. His account of this action appears in the chapter on the Hook battles later in this book.

Len Thompson replaced Sergeant Coveney as my troop sergeant and was one of the 2 Tp's rocks. I met up with him again at Bovington for the 80th Anniversary of the Battle of Cambrai attended by HM the Queen. As part of the programme, I was privileged to be given the job of showing her round the Korean section of the Tank Museum and could not resist bringing my scrap book to show her (not all of it!!). Many of the pictures were taken by Len and given to me, for which I am eternally grateful.

The author introducing Her Majesty the Queen to RTR Veterans at the Tank Museum. Sgt Len Thompson (2nd R) contributed many of the photos in this book, some of which were enjoyed by Her Majesty.

Sgts Coveney, Owens, Taylor and Phillips.

Lunch time break for the Troop.

Corporal Pearson.

Trooper Sharp.

Corporal Goldie.

Trooper Kelly.

Trooper 'Andy' Devine.

The author.

Trooper Griffin demonstates the new Remington razor on the front line. The company sent us free samples in the hope of gaining favourable publicity. I hope this plug is still of value to them!

Trooper Fenn was injured but returned to join a Tank Commander's Course I ran after the truce.

3 Troop head south over the Pintail Bridge on the way to the reserve area across the Imjin River.

*Above left*: Sergeant Len Thomson.

*Above right*: Corporal Pearson, and Troopers Bailey, Crabb and Bland.

# Chapter 3

# Life on the Line

## The Routine on the Frontline

After our first few days on the line relieving the Skins and meeting the Black Watch regiment we were supporting, my troop was nominated to rotate back for a fortnight with SHQ (Squadron Headquarters) in reserve. Each squadron, troop and even individuals, were continually rotating from reserve to different frontline positions and worked with and supported different units within the Division. Even to those present at the time, the movements were sometimes hard to keep abreast of. Over 70 years later, I am dependent on my photo album and memory to guide my account of these experiences.

In reserve, we helped to establish and trial the routes and movements for moving quickly to the front if needed. It wasn't until after Christmas that 2 Tp moved to tank positions on the front line to relieve 1 Tp at Point 187 and establish our fighting routines at the sharp end.

By this stage of the war, the function of these highly mobile, finely-tuned, 50 tonne technical marvels we called the Centurion, was reduced to a very expensive steel static pillbox. Each troop's tanks were positioned on the forward slopes of the front line, angled down so their main guns could be depressed to either fire into the valley and the approach slope if needed or elevated to fire into the Chinese positions across the valley on the opposing mountain side. Our tanks' positions were therefore in full view of the enemy and had to be protected from direct and indirect fire by their frontal armour (which was the strongest part of the Centurion), sandbag fortifications and earthworks.

The tanks had reserve positions, in dead ground and often only a few yards behind their firing points, where they could withdraw to and safely carry out essential maintenance, rearming ('bombing up') or refitting. Some

*Left*: One of the crew hoochies on Point 121.

*Below*: One of 3 Troop's Centurions on the line in the 'Elephant House'. This position was particularly exposed and required considerable defensive works to protect it. In this picture you can see tow ropes permanently secured to pull it out if there was a problem, and spare ammunition for the main gun on the engine decks. The four-man crew had a reasonably secure entry into the tank during crew changes. You can also see the telephone mounted on the rear for communicating with the crew inside when it was 'buttoned' up. Troopers Kirk, Devine, Rushman and Corporal Couzens pose for the cameras during a lull in the fighting.

firing points were exposed and vulnerable during day light and the tanks only moved into these points at dark. When this happened, the tanks would be driven back to their firing points, guided by pegs on the ground, so they were in their precise positions to resume their role. Precision was important because a few inches difference in positioning the Centurion would alter the aiming configuration and ruin the DF (Defensive Fire) effectiveness or even bring fire onto your own troops. These settings required three sighting shots on each target. In the event of a tank losing its position, the guns had to be re-zeroed and the entire DF charts (which might contain forty targets) recalculated and reregistered. Affixing the searchlight also altered the barrel's performance and might require re-zeroing. Sometimes, especially in the monsoon season, it was impossible to move the tanks because of the mud, even as far as their reserve position and they had to be rearmed in full view of the enemy.

A 3 Troop Centurion in its firing position, hull-down with the only turret (where its protection is strongest) exposed. After being 'stonked' (attracting enemy fire) during crew change overs, I built a screen of empty shell cases (on the left in this image) to cover the approaches from Chinese view.

The Centurion's engine also generated power for its electrical systems and since battery life was short, especially in the cold weather, the engines ran frequently. The turret could be power traversed rapidly and the main gun elevated and depressed with a hand wheel. The gunner, who sat on the right hand side of the main gun, had a traverse indicator dial marked off in degrees and an elevator indicator similarly marked which could be set at horizontal using a built-in spirit level. It was therefore possible to range on to an unseen target or in the dark, by setting these two instruments to the DF chart's data. Firing the main gun or the machine gun on these settings would match the impact zone of the registration shoot. Therefore, if the tank was moved and not returned to exactly the same position as during the initial registration, the tank was useless until recalibrated. It was important not to give the game away

This was a troop Hutchie just behind the crest and a short dash from the tanks. At any time 2 crew members would be in the tank, so the Hutchie might have to accommodate half of the troop. This was the troop's admin area where everything was done that couldn't be done in the tank.

when registering those defensive fire 'DF' targets so we would also have to fire several random decoy shells in different directions in the hopes of confusing the enemy.

Tanks were continuously manned, which necessitated all crews mounting a permanent watch in shifts. It also meant that each crew member had to be able to do every job on the tank, drive, load, fire the gun and operate the wireless. Each troop of four Centurion tanks remained fuelled, serviced and ready to move and could withdraw from its firing position into prearranged fallback positions. The tanks' engines were run regularly to keep the batteries charged since these were needed to run the radios and more importantly, the BV, or boiling vessel which kept the crew, much to the envy of our infantry colleagues, permanently supplied with boiling water for their tea and rations. On cold nights the engine running would also provide some warmth.

The troop command post, like other fighting and living positions on the front line, was called a 'hutchie', (or 'Hoochie' in the parlance of infantry units) and were either dugouts, burrowed into the ground if soft enough, or built up and fortified by sandbags and earthworks if not. These CPs were just behind the crests on the reverse slopes and although in dead ground, hidden from the enemy's direct view, were still susceptible to indirect artillery and therefore required overhead protection. Inside the CP were radios and maps for infantry and the tanks' commanders to coordinate the defence. Many of these hutchies could be sealed up from the inside in case the lines were overrun and on several occasions when this happened, soldiers inside waited for the Chinese to be evicted before re-emerging. In the Troop hutchies which were kept warm by petrol stoves, the crews took turns to sleep, wash, shave, cook and dry out. Soldiers were kept fit and warm carrying fuel, shells and Besa ammunition from the closest supply delivery point up to the firing points. On the line, the crews ate American field rations which included self-heating meals. Latrines were prepared by sappers a little further away, preferably down wind.

When we arrived, the Korean winter was in full swing and the Regiment had to acclimatise itself very quickly to the bitter cold after its voyage through tropical seas. It was very soon discovered that for the solitary watcher on the hill tops, no colder place could be found

*Above*: In December we took over from Mickey Farmer's 2 Troop (above) after a week in reserve.

*Below*: Tpr Fenn.

The Regiment tried to celebrate birthdays, even at the Front. The Cookhouse and the QM did us proud, sending cakes and beer when possible.

than a tank, which contrives to funnel the wind into its innermost parts and freezes its crew with the mass of cold metal in which they are enveloped. Amongst the many problems imposed by the cold, the cooking of breakfast was one of the most tiresome. All normal liquids were solid, eggs had to be peeled off their shells instead of broken and food had to be thawed before it could be fried. Milk was served with a knife.

When going on watch, the relieving crews faced the greatest danger because the Chinese knew our routines and understood this vulnerability. Each shift change attracted enemy attention and shell fire. The Centurion was boarded through the turret hatches and carried out in full view of the Chinese front. The replacement crew approached from the rear, using the tank as cover where possible and moving as quickly as possible to avoid sniper fire or inviting artillery. When the relief reached their tank, some used a telephone mounted on the rear of the tank to alert the crew inside that they were being replaced but some tanks also kept a hammer, attached by string, that was used to drum out a coded knock on the closed hatches so

'Bombing up'. One of the daily tasks was to restock the ammunition used the night before.

that the crews inside knew that it wasn't Chinese boarders. After a handover briefing, the crew being stood down would then dash back to the troop hutchies to avoid the inevitable incoming Chinese fire.

The Troop CPs were fed information on enemy movements from their tanks on the forward slopes a few metres away by field telephone. The troop CP was therefore behind the tank lines but integrated with the infantry fighting positions to aid communications and coordinate rapid support with the infantry. In the event of an attack by the Chinese PVA (People's Volunteer Army), apart from any forward patrols and OPs (observation points), the main body of infantry on the reverse slope would only engage the enemy once the tanks had been overrun. Therefore, the role of the tanks was to provide direct fire support on the advancing enemy and to call in artillery and air support to beat back the Chinese waves. On several occasions, Chinese assault troops used the static Centurions as cover during

In some positions, the tanks were pulled back from the line during the daylight. The crew could carry out their ablutions and restock and refuel in comparative safety. (Photo Denis Croft.)

attacks, sometimes sheltering underneath them from either their own, or our artillery which raked the positions.

It is important to explain that at this stage, the war had stabilised on what is now, 70 years later, still the boundary between North and South Korea. I have described the terrain as being like a flat board from which rows of hills of fairly even height have sprung, running very roughly east to west. Therefore, if one side captured a hill, it created a dent or a spur in the front line. At the end of 1952, the Commonwealth Division held commanding hilltop positions on hills such as 'Point 159', 'Point 210', 'The Hook', 'Yong Dong' and 'Hill 355' – Little Gibraltar. All these hills stuck out from the southern edge of the basic demarcation line between the opposing armies. Our role at the front was solely to support the infantry by providing direct (line of sight) fire, particularly at night. Throughout the day we scoured the enemy hillsides for any sign of movement and promptly fired at it with gratifying retribution from the Chinese artillery.

A typical 24 hour period could start with the radio in my tank crackling into life with a message from a British infantry patrol located in 'no man's land' that needed a distraction or was in trouble. The message would be something like 'Hello Bravo 2 – large Chinese patrol at Target T for Tommy 18. Fire cover needed'. I would reply 'Wilco Out' (Will comply!). Some 15 to 20 seconds later the sky would be lit up by the flashes of our main armament, the four 20 Pounder guns. 'Great. Thank you', would come the swift response from the infantry unit concerned. When this happened – and it did frequently, we had successfully fulfilled our role.

Perhaps worth mentioning is that Troop Commanders were given a lot of 'independence' in 'fighting' their Troops of 4 tanks. One of our Troop Leaders took the view that it was best to live and let live. In other words, if you didn't fire at the Chinese unless you had to, they wouldn't fire back. The benefit of this of course was that you avoided retaliatory fire and led a quieter life, but the other troop commanders all took the view that this was not consistent with our task of 'dominating no man's land'. Later in the war, it was publicly announced at a squadron parade by Capt. Arthur Thrift, 2IC (Administration) that 3 Troop had fired more shells at the Chinese than any other troop in the Squadron if not the whole regiment.

Indeed, it was only some years later that I became aware of the key outcome of this announcement by Capt. Thrift. This was my accelerated promotion to Battle Captain which was due to my and my troop's commitment to the task of dominating no man's land.

As mentioned, our tanks were dug in on the forward edges of the hills facing no man's land. They had to be far enough forward on the slope to

Arthur Thrift had had a very successful Second World War, like most of the soldiers in Korea that had served longer than seven years. He had emerged with a Military Cross and more experience than most. His commendation really meant something.

be able to depress their main guns and their machine guns into the valley and approach slopes. After 'stand to' at dusk and until 'stand to' at dawn, ('Stand to' was a two-hour period twice a day when all front line and rear echelon soldiers stood ready in case of an attack), two crew members remained on watch inside the tank and the other two rested in the hutchie or carried out Squadron tasks. The watches changed at midnight. On quiet days tanks might only have one crew member on watch per tank but were normally half manned and if events warranted it, they could be fully manned at a few moments' notice as we all slept fully dressed. Sometimes troops had reserve crew members in the hutchie who helped with ammunition restocking and crew relief.

In daylight the crew continually searched the Chinese lines on the other side of the valley. Any movement spotted immediately got the very accurate 20 pounders, the Centurion's main gun, traversed into a firing position. The number two in the turret loaded a high explosive shell into the breach of the gun shouting 'Loaded!' to which the Gunner replied 'Firing now' to be followed by a sort of whooshing noise and a clap of thunder as the shell left the gun. Machine gun fire from the Besa could add to the effect. Movement

Fire support from Point 121 onto deep Chinese positions. Enemy targets were identified by aerial reconnaissance, the mark 1 eyeball or counter-battery direction finding. Fire missions were often carried out in daylight and often within 30 seconds of being called for. We could post HE shells though a slit trench's 'window' at a mile's range.

My map showing 'B' sqn tank positions on the East of the Sami Chon River and the two main enemy gun positions that were our pet aversion. The 'H's mark the exact entrenched tank positions. The Hook positions are to the South West of this map.

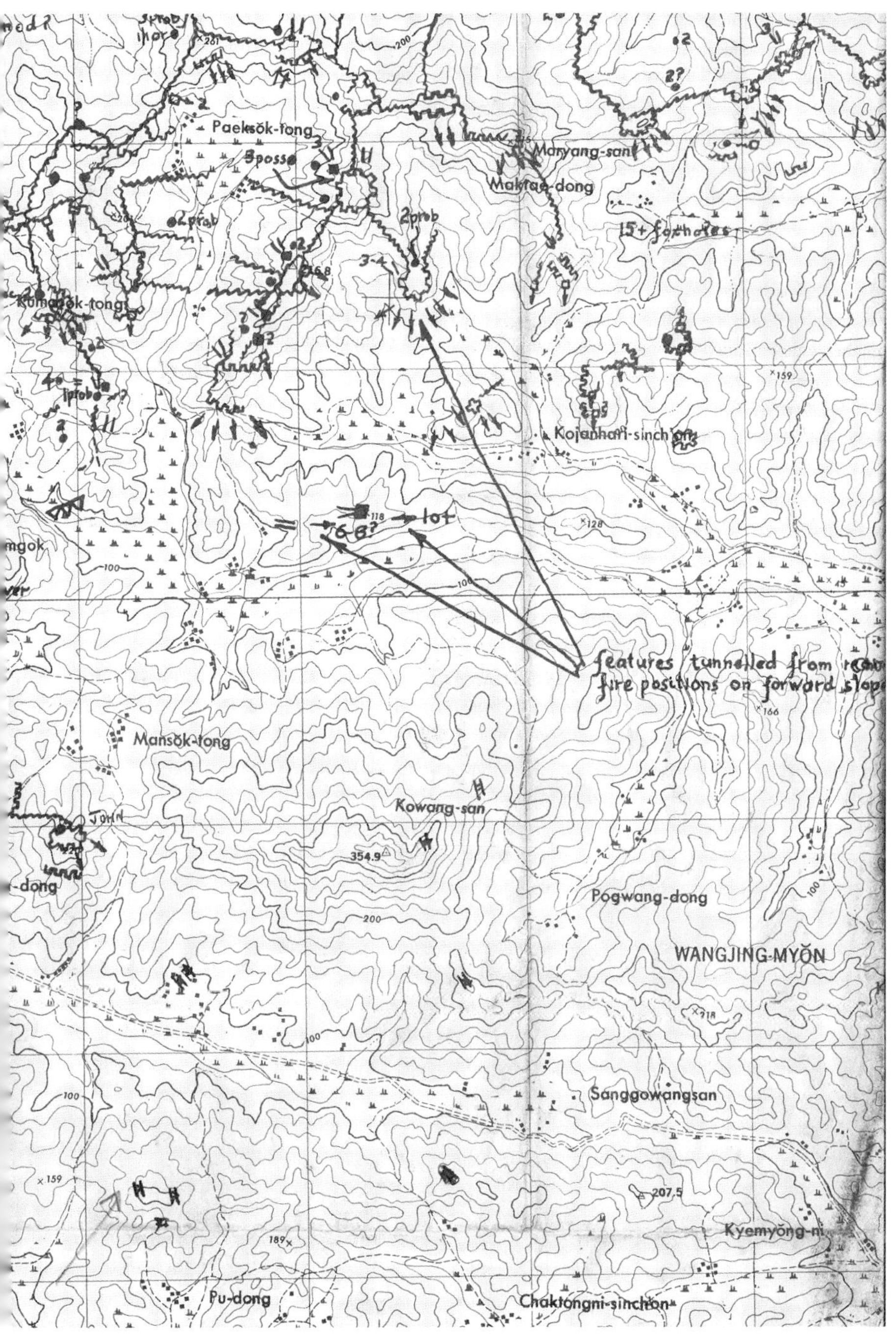
Paeksŏk-tong
Maryang-san
Maktae-dong
15+ foxholes
Kumgok-tong
Kojanhari-sinch'on
features tunnelled from rear
fire positions on forward slope
Mansŏk-tong
Kowang-san
354.9
Pogwang-dong
WANGJING-MYŎN
Sanggowangsan
207.5
Kyemyŏng-ni
Pu-dong
Chaktongni-sinch'on

was more often than not some poor Chinese conscript leaving his trench to use the latrines but we suppressed his sector without pity.

The success of the shoot could perhaps be best judged by the swiftness with which Chinese artillery returned the fire. The tank crews were reasonably safe, (throughout the tour only one member of the Regiment was killed and he wasn't in a Centurion at the time) and Chinese shells did not normally put a tank out of action. Enemy fire sometimes disabled moving parts such as the gun's elevation and depression ability or the optics but these were quickly repaired by the LAD fitters. Shells could also set fire to any material left on the decks or the electrics, as happened a few times. Certainly, they could leave scars on our armour plating and I was pleased that my tank sported several such 'scars' on its exterior! We felt this enemy fire to be 'irksome but ineffective' and depending on the speed and volume with which it was reciprocated by the Chinese, a reflection on our accuracy and impact on the enemy! Interestingly too, no infantryman ever complained (to me at least) about the retaliatory shellfire brought back on us by our many successes.

We were busiest at night. Neither side liked moving around in no man's land during daylight, so the days were spent preparing for the next night's

A crew performs a field service on a Centurion a short distance from its front line position.

darkness. The Centurions were infamous for guzzling fuel and most crews had to refill their tanks daily by hand. In most cases the tanks would reverse out of their positions and move a short distance into dead ground where the crew could service the engines and refuel and then return the tank to its exact position. Some positions were too exposed to man during daylight and these crews could withdraw a short distance to service the Cents in comparative safety.

The very first time we were fired at merits a mention. The story has a moral to it which may be of benefit to every soldier today. On the journey out in our troopship, my biggest worry was that when faced with enemy fire, my nerve would go and I would disgrace myself and my regiment. Thus, shortly after we had taken over in the line and the first shell suddenly landed close to our right rear, it was time to be tested. On this occasion, without further thought I commenced to prepare the obligatory 'Shell report'. While preparing this, I did notice Trooper Howarth, who had got married during our embarkation leave and was always happy to regale us with stories of his wedding and the subsequent nights of joy with his bride, shoot out of the 'bog' (latrine), trousers round his ankles, rushing for the safety of his tank. Afterwards he explained his inelegant reaction to the vital need to protect his marital equipment for his bride when they next met. However, a few minutes later, a second shell landed in the same general area. Calmly and coolly, I sent my 'second Shell report' on the regimental radio net. These were the first 'incomers' for the whole regiment. After a short pause, the adjutant's voice was heard over the regimental radio net enquiring rather sardonically whether I had seen today's regimental daily instructions. These included a notice that the Royal Engineers would be blasting latrine holes in the frozen ground nearby that very morning. The egg on my face did little to dim the huge relief when I realised I had not panicked under shell fire – of course it wasn't actual shellfire but I had thought it was! It was a boost to my self confidence and as a story, may give confidence to any young soldiers who have not yet had battle experience. Somehow you don't panic when the chips are down!!!

Here I must add that though in retrospect our time in Korea turned out to be fun, while 'in the line', our lives were at risk 24/7. Clambering in and out over the rear of the Centurion in full view (and small arms range) of the enemy invariably drew their attention and you could always expect to be 'stonked' by observant Chinese riflemen or gunners as you slithered down to the ground. At night on watch, there was the obvious risk that Chinese snatch patrols could creep up and kill you or drag you back to China. I always slept with a sharp bayonet by my side ready to fight my way out of my sleeping bag should I be attacked by an aggressive Chinese patrol that had slipped silently through our lines in the dark. I had a particular fear of being zipped up to the neck in my sleeping bag by said patrol and carried off kicking and screaming into the night helpless to do anything about it. Also, when driving to headquarters or to the reserve areas, or even for those (including the KSC) delivering supplies, there were stretches of road that were visible to Chinese gunners who would fire at the telltale dust vehicles kicked up, hoping, and sometimes succeeding, in hitting the vehicle. (This was how Trooper Dixon, the Regiment's only fatality, was killed.) On top

*Above, opposite above and opposite below*: Note the 'Tugs' – a turret-less Centurion, callsign 'Starlight' used for armoured logistical tasks, troop movement and casualty movement near the front. After a few months on the front line, the Division was rotated into reserve and a US Army Division replaced us. When they moved into our fighting positions we brought all our vehicles and equipment across the Imjin River to our reserve positions in Gloucester Valley.

of that there were many minefields left by the Chinese when they were forced out of an area. On one occasion I came across several KSC porters badly wounded and trapped in an unmarked mine field. Hardly anywhere was totally safe and most of us had farewell letters stuck up in our hutchies to our loved ones back home.

## Casualty evacuation

In the event of taking a casualty (and 1 RTR was relatively lucky to have had only 1 soldier killed and around 20 wounded) there were well-drilled systems to evacuate casualties. Injured tank crews could be driven to the aid posts in their tanks and then unloaded. This happened a few times but because it involved taking a tank off the line, it was only done if the tank was inoperable. Otherwise, casualties could be retrieved by the 'tugs', turretless Centurion hulls which provided a protective ride to the aid stations. Once at the aid station, triage separated those who could be treated locally and those who needed to be flown out by helicopter, an emerging battlefield medical transportation, to the hospital ships or the main military hospitals near Seoul.

I was a 'casualty' myself at one point, though not by enemy action. I had an ingrown toenail that needed an operation to remove. Much to my embarrassment, I was hospitalised, the first in the Regiment – and probably the Brigade. The surgical team at the divisional hospital threatened to keep me for a fortnight so I had to call Dick Ward to be released immediately after the operation. The squadron enjoyed my discomfort and produced a cartoon which gently elevated the severity of this minor incapacitation into a purple heart citation from General Clark, the Senior UN Commander.

*Above, opposite above and opposite below*: Helicopters were in wide use for the first time and were particularly effective in casualty evacuation. A casualty on the front line could be treated on a hospital ship within 30 minutes, This represented miraculous progress to the veterans and made a huge difference to survivability.

RESCUE

## Working with Infantry

During the long cold nights that followed, we supported infantry patrols sent out to meet and fight any Chinese patrols or even assault Chinese positions. This was a part of dominating no man's land. Preparation for these actions involved our registering tank fire, either shells or machine gun fire, on selected points and logging the settings.

Thus, if during the night, a patrol called us for fire support on the radio 'Fire Tommy 6!', we could put down the appropriate shell or machine gun fire on the given spot within 20 seconds. Alternatively, enemy infantry could be dealt with with a call for 'Besa' and 'Tulip', in which case the turret mounted searchlight would turn on and the machine gun would clear an area of illuminated enemy.

Our role at the front was to provide support and protection to whichever infantry unit was located at the points we were posted to and help them to 'dominate' no man's land. In return, they supported us from forward observation positions and protected our rear. Over the coming months on the front line, this allowed us to work closely and compare the performance and

The mainstay of infantry positions were the sited machine guns. These could lay down fire along prearranged arcs or engage opportune targets as they appeared.

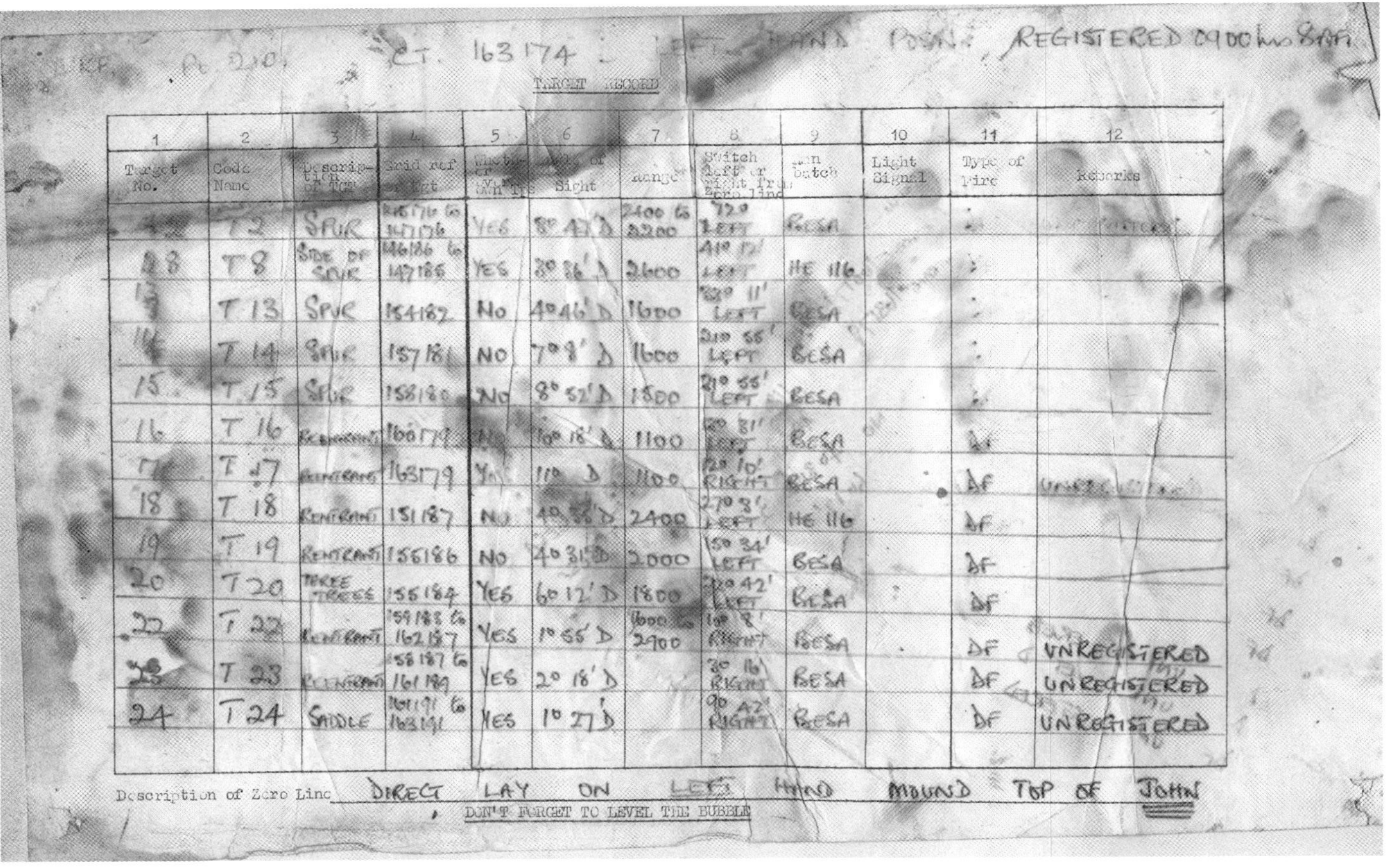

RF Pt 210, CT. 163174 : LEFT HAND POSN. REGISTERED 0900 hrs [illegible]

TARGET RECORD

| 1 | 2 | 3 | 4 | 5 | 6 | 7 | 8 | 9 | 10 | 11 | 12 |
|---|---|---|---|---|---|---|---|---|---|---|---|
| Target No. | Code Name | Description of Tgt | Grid ref of Tgt | [illegible] | [illegible] of Sight | Range | Switch Left or Right from Zero line | [illegible] Batch | Light Signal | Type of Fire | Remarks |
| 2 | T 2 | SPUR | 145176 to 147176 | YES | 8° 47' D | 2400 to 2200 | 72° LEFT | BESA | | | [illegible] |
| 8 | T 8 | SIDE OF SPUR | 146186 to 147186 | YES | 3° 36' D | 2600 | 41° 12' LEFT | HE 116 | | | |
| 13 | T 13 | SPUR | 154182 | No | 4° 46' D | 1600 | 38° 11' LEFT | BESA | | | |
| 14 | T 14 | SPUR | 157181 | NO | 7° 8' D | 1600 | 21° 55' LEFT | BESA | | | |
| 15 | T 15 | SPUR | 158180 | NO | 8° 52' D | 1500 | 21° 55' LEFT | BESA | | | |
| 16 | T 16 | RE-ENTRANT | 160179 | NO | 10° 18' D | 1100 | 20° 31' LEFT | BESA | | DF | |
| 17 | T 17 | RE-ENTRANT | 163179 | YES | 11° D | 1100 | 12° 10' RIGHT | BESA | | DF | UNREGISTERED |
| 18 | T 18 | RE-ENTRANT | 151187 | NO | 4° 36' D | 2400 | 27° 8' LEFT | HE 116 | | DF | |
| 19 | T 19 | RE-ENTRANT | 155186 | NO | 4° 31' D | 2000 | 15° 34' LEFT | BESA | | DF | |
| 20 | T 20 | THREE TREES | 155184 | YES | 6° 12' D | 1800 | 20° 42' LEFT | BESA | | DF | |
| 22 | T 22 | RE-ENTRANT | 159183 to 162187 | YES | 1° 55' D | 1600 to 2900 | 10° 8' RIGHT | BESA | | DF | UNREGISTERED |
| 23 | T 23 | RE-ENTRANT | 158187 to 161189 | YES | 2° 18' D | | 3° 16' RIGHT | BESA | | DF | UNREGISTERED |
| 24 | T 24 | SADDLE | 161191 to 163191 | YES | 1° 27' D | | 9° 42' RIGHT | BESA | | DF | UNREGISTERED |

Description of Zero Line DIRECT LAY ON LEFT HAND MOUND TOP OF JOHN

DON'T FORGET TO LEVEL THE BUBBLE

DF (Direct Fire) Sheet from the Tp Leader's position on Pt 210 (Some are marked on the photo of the enemy positions overleaf).

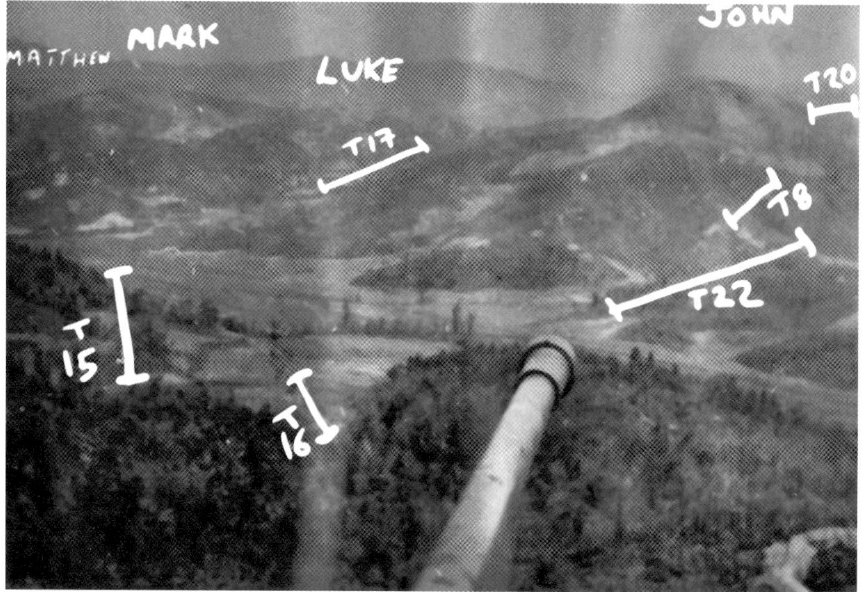


The 'Apostles'. The view of enemy positions at hills Matthew, Mark, Luke and John from Pt 210. My markings are the Defensive Fire impact zones from the DF list on the previous pages.

attitudes of many units including the Black Watch, the King's Regiment, the Royal Fusiliers, the Canadian 'Vingt Douze', two Australian Battalions of the RAR, the Royal Scots, the Durham Light Infantry, the Duke of Wellington's, the US Marines and a Turkish infantry unit. What I found fascinating was that each regiment had its own characteristics and a uniquely aggressive stance or energy towards fulfilling this role. Sadly, some units were more effective at shaping no man's land and defending the positions than others.

A company of one infantry battalion, that shall remain nameless, was humiliated by the Chinese and their sloppy sentry work and failure to dominate no man's land resulted in the Chinese posting Christmas cards on their frontline positions.

It was astonishing to see that the Australians who took over from them managed to re-dominate no man's land within 48 hours. They booby trapped the wire so the Chinese stopped posting cards and launched an aggressive patrol policy deep into no man's land. Within 48 hours the Chinese no longer dared to cross the valley floors yet alone climb up our side of the hills. Well done the Aussies!

'The Chinese posted Christmas cards containing propaganda messages on the barbed wire in front of the more relaxed UN forward positions. Dear Soldiers, it is Christmas and you are far from home, suffering from cold not knowing when you will die. The big shots are home enjoying themselves, eating good food, drinking good liquor, why should you be here risking your life for their profits?

The Koreans and Chinese don't want to be your enemies. Our enemies and yours are those that sent you here and destroyed your happiness. Let's join hands! You belong back home with those who love you and want you back, safe and sound. So we wish you greetings from the Chinese People's Volunteers.'

The Centurions were sited so that they could depress their main armament into the valley and defend the approach slopes against enemy infantry, as well as being able to provide fire support on any movement in the Chinese lines. Bill Skinner of 2 Royal Australian Regiment swaps his hole in the ground for a gentleman's view over no man's land and Chinese lines.

It wasn't only the Commonwealth forces that had units with poor reputations. Our neighbours until February, the US Marines, ran a tight line and were happy to have us as neighbours; there were no defensive works between us since we were mutually confident neither force would allow the Chinese to get between us and into our flanks. But the first thing the US Marines did when we were pulled back into reserve and replaced by the US Army was to secure their mutual boundary with wire post and mines. We chose to take this as a discreet compliment from the US marines.

## The tale of a Chinaman's Surrender

One night, the Duke of Wellington's were doing a Snatch patrol to capture a Chinese lookout who had been seen to return to the same position at dusk each night. Our plan was to provide distractive shellfire to offset any noise made by the Snatch patrol and to keep adjacent Chinese heads down. Once the patrol secured a prisoner we were to provide cover fire on fixed spots to prevent the patrol being followed on their return.

It appeared to us that all had gone very well and it was confirmed the next morning that our support fire had been extremely successful. The only fly in the ointment we were told was that when the patrol pounced on the hapless Chinaman, he kept shouting something in Chinese. 'Shut up' they hissed but the more they clipped the poor man round the ear, the more he shouted this expression. This commotion was seriously threatening the safety of the mission so to hush him up, they gagged him with a sock and some sticking tape over his mouth. When we reported this to the debriefing intelligence officer, he burst out laughing. 'The poor guy was only shouting "I surrender"'. Later that morning the Chinaman received a chocolate, cigarettes and an apology from the snatch team.

Sadly 70 years later I was unable to corroborate this story with the DWR but I would like to feel that it was logged into their official records since the 1st Tanks War diary shows the number of shells we fired in support that night and the praise received from them. I distinctly remember gearing up for it and firing the covering rounds – and I am pretty sure the name of the patrol leader was David Gilbert Smith but as mentioned, sadly the DWR have no official record of it!

For our part, I also recall my Squadron received formal praise which was promptly passed on to me. This episode marked the beginning of the subtle improvement in my relationship with Major Ward and indeed I was later advised that he approved of 3 Troop's aggressive attitude. Certainly, my relationship with Major Ward which had started on such a very low ebb, improved visibly to herald a lifelong friendship.

## On Patrol with 1 RAR

In the meantime, our support for the appropriate local infantry Battalion continued to be appreciated, though in the case of the Australians, with one most unusual result. One Major Bill Skinner, a tough, wiry and very aggressive company commander, seemed to enjoy winding me up at every opportunity, referring to me as that typical British 'Pom'. It seemed simplest to appear unfazed by this baiting, so I slipped into feigning a drawling Pom accent. But I went too far one day by saying in my posh drawl that I'd never been so bored as fighting besides these ex convicts.

'Oh Pom', he replied, 'if you've nothing to do, you can come on patrol with me tonight'.

Gulping, I managed to reply with as much nonchalance as I could muster, 'Yes of course, if you need my help'. But it was definitely round one to the Aussies!

On this occasion I went back to my tanks and commenced feverish activity. Firstly, I ensured they all registered appropriate defensive fire targets to cover the route we were expected to take down to the valley and back. Of course, I couldn't tell Dick Ward as he would unquestionably stop

Point 210 was one of the troop positions manned by 1 RTR to support the 2nd Battalion The Royal Australian Regiment and we had a hectic but successful time. Major Bill Skinner, the local Australian Company Commander, won one of our many verbal battles by leaving me no option but to go out on a night recce with him – I ensured maximum tank support for this daring operation!

me going. I wrote a farewell note to my widowed father and stuck it up on my dugout wall. Hoping I looked cool and calm, I tried to imitate Field Marshall Montgomery by getting some sleep just as he did before the Battle of El Alamein, but I'm afraid to say, in this I failed.

At the appropriate time I turned up for the pre-patrol briefing and was issued with a Sten submachine gun, grenades and ammunition. I was told I would be 'tail end Charlie' and that if the patrol went to ground, I was to face the rear and see that we were not attacked from behind.

We set off, about 10 of us, with the Major leading. About two thirds of the way down to the valley there was a quiet hiss and everyone went flat on the ground. I faced the rear for several minutes, concentrating on ensuring nobody was attacking from that direction. Then suddenly a heavy hand shook my shoulder. I froze. This was the end! But to my embarrassment it was the hand of a friendly Ozzy who informed me that the rest of the patrol had moved on ages ago. Feeling sheepish, I caught up with the others and took up a defensive observation position with them down in the valley. After some time, I received a whispered message that an enemy patrol had been seen on the patrol's infrared gunsight. It was too large for us and we were not to fire at it unless they fired first. As we lay there silently, they passed us by and after about an hour, the Major decided we would return to our base.

As we wound our way back up the hill, I whispered to the Major that it might just give him confidence for the future if my tanks did a practice

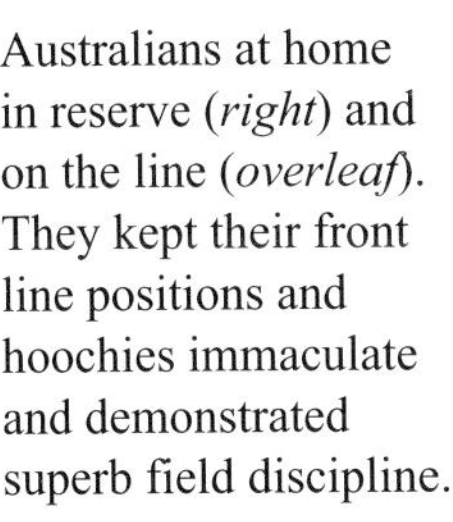

Australians at home in reserve (*right*) and on the line (*overleaf*). They kept their front line positions and hoochies immaculate and demonstrated superb field discipline.

defensive fire shoot. 'Oh, go on Pom, if you must play at soldiers.' I passed the whispered instructions over the radio to my tanks to fire on the appropriate DF targets a few yards from our position. The patrol carried on up the hill and about 20 seconds later, the sky around us lit up with the flashes and thunder of our four big guns. The result was something better than I had ever dreamt of! The speed with which the Major and his patrol hit the deck was better than in any Hollywood movie. As I stood above him with my hands on my hips, I gleefully relished his come-uppance. 'It's all right Major, you've got nothing to worry about. It's only my tanks covering our withdrawal."

Australian Infantry about to go out on patrol. Trenches cut through the crest protected the patrols from being 'sky-lined' when they went forward of the positions at dusk.

I ensured maximum tank support for the daring operation. Day or night we could fire along predesignated trajectories and bearings, hitting targets that we couldn't see either in the dark or through smoke.

It was good to think that the mother country always won the last round! Certainly, there was less Pommy bashing but equally I should stress that my admiration and respect for the Aussies was uncompromising. On this occasion however, it was 'game, set and match' to the Poms!!

# Chapter 4

# In Reserve

The Regiment was usually structured to maintain a strength of two squadrons in the line with one 'resting' in reserve. Normally, the troops in reserve faced a softer and less hazardous routine than those on the front line but the workload and training didn't let up. The troops would be administered and managed from their Squadron Headquarters which were located a few miles behind the front line, just out of the range of Chinese artillery. When the troop was rotated out of the line, a replacement troop from the Regiment would take over the troop's position and get briefed by the departing troop on the active situation. The relieved troop would then head to the Squadron area in reserve. These were more than merely opportunities to unwind after the rigours of the frontline; they also gave us the opportunity to educate the

A view from the top of 'Gloucester Hill' of Castle Hill and across the Imjin Valley towards the North.

The top of Gloucester Hill.

infantry on our capabilities and share our lessons, procedures and tactics with the other squadrons.

Reserves were still expected to maintain a state of readiness to move rapidly to reinforce parts of the line if required and this required us to learn and practise the routes to the positions we might have to reinforce at a moment's notice. Sometimes, support fire was required by infantry which the dug-in Centurions could not bear their guns on, so tanks would be brought up from reserve to cover these fire missions. We had to know what the contingency plans were for the worst case scenario, which was a Chinese breakthrough, especially around the Hook area, which would open up the Imjin Valley and Seoul (not to mention my personal belongings and souvenirs in our reserve area!) to the Chinese and necessitate a fighting withdrawal. It was unlikely this would happen, the lines had been stagnant for a while but the Chinese had advanced rapidly over this same route a couple of years earlier and had not given up hope of repeating this battlefield success. However, we were confident that our training in Germany had prepared us for this rear guard action and we doubted the Chinese would risk a nuclear confrontation which the Americans were beginning to use as a threat to hurry along the peace talks.

There were a number of different reserve positions, starting with the immediate reserve which was close to the front line and required crews to

Pintail Bridge, a key bridge between the reserve areas and the front lines.

We trained hard to move in all weather conditions. The Troop spent its first stint in reserve practising movement across the frozen hills before moving up to the immediate reserve behind Pt 159. Later we practised in monsoon conditions.

be on standby to move to the front line. We then had the Squadron reserve area where we lived when we were in reserve. We had reserve fall back fighting positions pencilled in behind the Imjin River and we spent time siting prospective defensive positions and moving to them. We also recced and practised possible counter attack options.

This necessitated a number of squadron- and regiment-level exercises and working with the units we would be supporting. There were also one or two missions or raids planned when tanks would accompany infantry on specific operations and these required rehearsals and close cooperation between the units. A few of these raids were carried out with mixed success and it was always a hope that our troop would have an opportunity to fight the tanks the way they were designed to be fought.

There were constant reminders that a Chinese advance should not be discounted or underestimated. In their initial invasion of South Korea, this was the exact axis of advance and breakthrough point they had taken as they rolled southwards. WW2 era Chinese and North Korean tanks and other wrecked vehicles lay where they had been destroyed.

Rehearsing moves to reinforce or reposition the squadron needed to include familiarisation of different conditions and seasons. For instance, in the rainy season, the water flowed over these bridges and the approaches (and even some roads) were impassible. In the summer, we could ford the river at more convenient locations.

The extreme weather conditions in Korea played havoc with these operations and our plans and contingencies had to be reassessed

River levels changed every week. Where they might be forded one day, they could be flooded or frozen the next.

An abandoned and damaged Russian T34 tank that had not fared well in the technology mismatch following the initial invasion through the Imjin Valley. Most equipment used by the North Korean and Chinese forces was former Soviet WW2 era.

continually. Heavy rain in the monsoon season could make some routes impossible to travel along, even with the tracked vehicles, and ice could make other routes impassable. Heavy rain also flooded the rivers and made them unfordable for weeks. Even some of the bridges which were designed to let the flood waters pass over them, could not be used at these times. Alternative routes and positions had to be established and practised.

## Routine and Administration in Reserve

In addition to these defensive and offensive possibilities, there were routine jobs that were carried out in reserve areas. These included taking supplies up to the troops on the front line and visiting crews. Sometimes, extra personnel were taken to the fighting positions to bolster the crew numbers.

Heading back down to Gloucester Valley from our forward positions (Top) and forwarding the Imjin River. (Below) Fording the Imjin was possible at certain times. We crossed the river a few times, once when we were replaced on the line by the US forces for a break in the spring and then back a few months later when we returned to our positions on the front.

Rehearsing to reinforce or reposition the squadron during different conditions and seasons. For instance, in the rainy season, the water flowed over these bridges. In the Summer, we could ford or bridge the river at more convenient locations.

After a heavy night on the line resupplies, such as ammunition and fuel, might need to be taken to the tank positions, often carried the last few hundred yards up the steep slopes since vehicles could not get close. Approaching the fighting positions often involved travelling along access routes in full view of Chinese observers and being exposed to their artillery which had our routes and positions registered for artillery bombardment in the same way we did to them.

The Squadron leader would visit the troops on the front line every day and I would often accompany him to visit friends and catch up on news. We would often bring up surplus crew members to ease the workload and administration of the four-man crews at the sharp end. They would help by preparing meals, loading ammunition, cleaning weapons and joining sentry rosters, allowing the crew commanders more time to improve their positions, liaise with their local infantry commanders or carry out registration shoots.

*Above and below*: What better team building exercise than using the Squadron's combined resources to relocate the Sqn Leader's caravan?

In the squadron reserve area, there were endless jobs to be done, improving and fixing the lines and maintaining the vehicles there. The squadron HQ and the reserve squadron tanks were kept operational and used for exercises, and in many ways the routine at war resembled that of the Regiment's peacetime role in Germany. Lots of maintenance, lots of administrative tasks and lots of sports, some jobs challenged our resources. One 'command task' took a full squadron and its vehicles to move the squadron leader's caravan onto a ridge.

With the tactical administrative obligations met, the army appreciated that men needed to unwind and offered more entertaining diversions and opportunities to escape from the stresses of the front line.

Being in reserve gave us a rare opportunity to spend time with members of the Regiment not in our own troop. The front line was hectic and divided one's attention from the human aspect of the regiment.

Moving tanks was rarely done except while in reserve, however we brought them down when the Americans relieved us in February and returned them in April, and we sometimes moved along roads in convoys to exercise areas. In those instances we worked with other units like the Military Police and even the Royal Navy to avoid problems with locals or neighbouring units.

*Above and left*: In the first Winter we brought the Cents down across the Imjin for the Division's turn in reserve. It was times like this we thanked God we didn't have to walk, like the PBI.

## Relaxation

Despite a war in full swing a few miles away, there were aspects of surreal normality in our routines, particularly in terms of taking weekends. When in reserve we were often worked less hard on Sundays and in some cases released for the entire weekend. Often there would be voluntary (but 'heavily-encouraged') church parades on Sunday mornings and then soldiers were allowed to leave the bases and either go into Seoul or relax at rest centres by the Imjin River. On days off, truckloads of our soldiers were taken to the River where we swam, played water sports, fished and generally relaxed. It was here, over time, I developed a passion for dinghy sailing.

An off-duty soldier could get a meal and a drink at a number of NAAFI roadhouses, like the Newmarket Roadhouse or the Ship Inn. There was also a remarkable Mobile Laundry and Bath Unit service. It was like a conveyor belt. You stripped off at one end and handed in your dirty clothing, went through a very efficient shower and were handed fresh clothing on the other side. These units didn't separate ranks or nations and on one occasion

There were plenty of streams and pools where we could swim and relax. Uniform standards were relaxed.

*Above and left*: The NAAFI offered soldiers some home comforts in their road houses.

*Above and below*: Traditional sports like football and cricket helped soldiers unwind from the line.

*Above, below and opposite*: Less familiar sports, such as baseball and basketball, introduced by our US neighbours, also took place on the squadron's playing field.

I found myself standing naked next to a giant African American towering over me. He looked down at me and said in a heavy Southern drawl 'Hey you, scrub ma back'. Frankly it did not seem the time or the place to argue or pull rank – so I complied and he returned the compliment by scrubbing mine! After this I always took my batman (an orderly) with me on subsequent visits and made him salute me so there would be no more doubt or familiarity in the shower!

Sport was the best way to unwind after the intensity of being on the front line and matches and sports afternoons were regularly organised, as if at home. Important fixtures between units sometimes involved bringing talented players out of the line for the duration of the match. Regiments like the Dukes prided themselves on their rugby prowess and proved hard to beat, even with your best players temporarily pulled from the line and beefed up with Kiwis and Aussies on loan!

Reserve duty might have felt less important, but after work or sport, there were regular meals in the mess tent or the Officers' Mess, hot water and at least we slept in clean bedding under canvas.

*Above and below*: After living in hutchies and cold steel on the front line and sleeping though artillery and the ever-present threat of attack, living in and operating from tents seemed luxurious.

## Normality

It might seem strange to observers that so much time was dedicated to sport in the Army, especially during wartime, but all the best leaders I knew promoted sport and understood its importance, especially in the stressful environment we were in. Good units ensured that the men were fit and happy and worked well together. Team sports in particular achieved all of these and good leadership recognised the value of normality. In fact, our time in reserve was run as if we were in barracks in a peace time army in Germany or Britain, working, whenever possible, only in the morning, with plenty of sport and relaxation afterwards. This not only improved morale but allowed soldiers to truly decompress from the battlefield. It helped soldiers process the conflict and would have long-term beneficial effects on the mental welfare of veterans. Consequently, the brigade built sports facilities in the reserve area and our squadron had its own football pitch and cricket oval!

Being in reserve was undoubtedly safer than being in the front but never entirely so. A brother officer, Michael Colston, (later of Colston dishwasher

A concert party near the Front. This entertainment was organised by the New Zealand contingent.

fame) was a memorable character who exemplified the difference between our American counterparts and the Commonwealth forces, and their different attitudes towards health and safety at work. A national serviceman loaned to us from the 17/21 Lancers, Michael's character is perhaps best summed up with a story about his last few days in Korea.

Fellow RTR officers Mike Colston (left) with Simon Agnew. Mike's final mission in Korea was to escort an American Colonel on a tour of the front lines.

The Imjin River by Widgeon Ferry. This was the Weekend Leave Centre at Inchon. It was only a short drive away from the front lines but a different world. The Ferry in action, carrying troops to and from the Leave centre.

*Above and below*: Whenever possible, truckloads of our soldiers went across (sometimes by ferry) to the Imjin River where we swam, played water polo and generally relaxed.

For his final days as a National Serviceman, he had been transferred to regimental headquarters to await 'demob' (demobilisation). An American Colonel visiting the HQ at this time expressed a wish to view the British frontline. 'Sure, nothing easier' said Colonel Gerry and asked Mike to drive the visitor round the frontline areas in an open Jeep.

Before setting off, the American paused to put on full body armour including a flak jacket and steel helmet, placing a carbine across his knees.

Seeing Mike only armed with a pistol and casually wearing his jersey and beret, the Colonel was clearly embarrassed and said to Mike 'You'll have to forgive me but I'm due for a posting home in three months. I have to be careful. How about you? How long have you got before demob?'

'I go tomorrow!' Mike replied. The mortified Yank Colonel could only mumble 'Gee, you guys sure must trust your frontline troops!'

## Training with the Durham Light Infantry

Often individual troops were rotated for short breaks from the line but in January 1953, the Americans relieved the entire 1st Commonwealth Division sector until April and 1 RTR moved to their assigned reserve area in Gloucester Valley for an extended 'rest'. When we went into reserve, there were busy schedules for training and opportunities to build

Training with the DLI involved familiarising them with our tanks' capabilities. Following this attachment, we moved back up to the line to relieve the US brigade. Here 4 Tp move up to the Front with supplies loaded on the engine decks.

relations between neighbouring and supported units. These might include familiarising infantry units with tank doctrine or conducting combined arms exercises.

There was also an assortment of challenging troop and squadron tasks to fulfil. After lots of inspections, maintenance and training, B squadron were dispatched to train with 28 Brigade. Each troop was attached to a separate battalion and 2 Tp was attached to the Durham Light Infantry (DLI) for two weeks at their camp at George Hill.

Again, a state of war wasn't going to interfere with the niceties of army life and we attended a battalion parade where over 1000 troops bade farewell to the brigade commander, Tom Daly, a few hundred yards beyond Chinese artillery range.

In reserve, we frequently invited infantry aboard the tanks and if the opportunity occurred, got them to sight the gun and fire at a target. The 20 pounder gun was incredibly accurate at a mile and we could hit man-sized targets at that range. When we got the infantry to do this, it gave them immense confidence in the support we could give them.

The brigade held a farewell parade for its departing Brigadier and for a few hours, over a thousand Commonwealth soldiers stood around in a bunch, just beyond the reach of Chinese artillery. The Brigade forms up at Camp George. The Durham Light Infantry march past at the double, followed by the 1st Royal Tank Regiment. The Royal Australian Regiment march past and take the salute.

*Above*: The Durham Light Infantry even brought their bugles with them to Korea.

*Below and opposite above*: The Durham Light Infantry even brought their buglers to Korea.

Bob MacGregor-Oakford at Camp George.

Brigadier R. MacGregor-Oakford of the DLI, then a 2nd lieutenant, said that on the 14th April 1953, he had been leading a small night recce patrol in no man's land when he and his patrol stumbled across a large Chinese outpost. He immediately called on the Tanks for prearranged defensive fire support and he and his men were extremely relieved when, within 20 seconds, 20 pounder shells rained down on the Chinese outpost permitting Bob and his men to pull back to safety. Long after the war, Bob was kind enough to say that the support came from my tank – but I don't recall if it was mine. This was a routine fire mission and doesn't stand out in my memory – but I am confident that it was one of my troop – probably a Centurion located on the left hand forward slopes of Hill 355.

For sure all my troop took pride in giving such swift support. What was welcome was his comment that without that prompt and very effective fire support, he and his patrol might well have been killed or captured. On another occasion Sgt Jim Murray, BEM of the DLI, vividly described

Intense training with the DLI prepared us for a mobile phase which never materialised. However, our time together developed trust and respect which served us well in the line together. Here Sgt Coveney and the remainder of 'B' Sqn carry out more exercises as Spring thawed the hills and paddy fields.

Major Johnny Tresawna and some of his company after an exercise. Johnny was killed at the Hook on the 10th June 1953 and we visited his grave in the UN cemetery in Pusan before we left for Suez.

The DLI were nothing if not resourceful. The 'flying box' on Hill 355, was built to carry supplies, ammunition and even casualties from the hill tops to the valley supply points.

the fierce fighting that occurred during the war and expressed his praise and thanks to our tanks for their swift support .

I didn't know him, but General Sir Peter de la Billiere served with the 1st Battalion DLI in Korea as a nineteen year old officer in the positions we supported and lived alongside our own hutchies in similar conditions which he described perfectly in his book *Looking for Trouble: SAS to Gulf Command.*

The good relations between the 1st Tanks and the DLI strengthened during my troop's training secondment to the DLI. Their tough Geordie resilience, quick wittedness and a marvellous sense of humour made them a joy to work with. Writing about them in *The Observer* at the time, Patrick O'Donovan described the DLI as:

> *...small, cheerful, slightly disrespectful men who were at their best when things were most beastly and who would go home*

We practised infantry / tank cooperation and got lots of value from this. We let them drive our tanks and fire our guns. As a testament to the survivability of the Centurion, this tank survived the experience! Their resourcefulness could be challenging at times but fortunately the six Geordies in my Troop (Andy Devine, Sgt Kelly and Corporal Fenn among them) provided a 'shield of brotherhood' that protected my troop from the DLI's 'scrounging'; the remainder of the Division had to nail everything down!

The author at Camp George after the parade. Even during the war and within earshot of the enemy artillery, they had found time to paint each stone around the parade square!

> *to vote as far left as they could. There was a singular lack of military nonsense about them and yet they were so professional that they made their neighbours, the United States Marines, look like amateurs.*

Had the Korean War resorted to a more mobile phase, the training we did with them would have been invaluable. I think both sides were very sad when we returned to our own lines and indeed their commanding officer,

Lt Col Peter Jeffreys DSO OBE, wrote a charming letter to Colonel Gerry about the value of our visit which I shamelessly kept!

My time in Korea has left me with huge respect for the Geordies. If you are ever in trouble, you can always rely on them to help get you out of it!

## Trip to the aircraft carrier

John Damant was an irrepressibly bright, intelligent and genial subaltern, loaned to us from the 7th Hussars, and later on in the war was attached as ADC to the Divisional Commander. He was an ideal nominee to fill this vacancy but his inability to resist playing pranks let him down on several occasions. One ended with his return to our mess with his tail between his legs bemoaning the fact that the General did not possess a sense of humour.

Once he had settled in as ADC, he noticed the two-wheeled caravan trailer his boss slept in was parked beside a deep shell hole filled with water. Looking for something to do to fill up some dull moments in respect of the war situation, John hit on an idea. While the General was asleep, he quietly turned the trailer round 180° so that the door opened directly onto the shell hole. He then drove one of the Headquarters' defence Centurions stealthily forward until its barrel was level with the trailer. Having elevated the gun, he pointed it at the Chinese lines, loaded a shell and fired. The poor General shot out of his bunk, hastily exited his trailer and came to rest up to his waist in water.

On returning to the regiment the next morning, a very melancholy John told us he just couldn't understand why his boss hadn't seen the funny side! Clearly his sense of fun was always very close to the surface.

On the way out to Korea in our troopship, we had anchored offshore in Colombo and gone ashore. On the way back to the ship, we noticed a military attaché's car from the Soviet Union unattended on the dockside, its Red Star pennant fluttering. The Attaché was further on down the quay studying the troopship through his binoculars.

Climbing back onboard the *Halladale*, John proudly pulled out that same pennant from his pocket. A little later as the *Halladale* started to get underway, we were surprised to find the ship slowing down again. Eventually the engines stopped altogether and she hove to. Immediately

John Damant, 7th Hussars, on secondment to B Sqn1RTR.

John and I were sent on a liaison trip to the British aircraft carrier, HMS *Ocean*. We were flown out by the US Navy in Grumman Avengers.

*Above and below*: The aircraft carrier looked too small to land on.

US aircraft carrier, the *Bairoko* under steam as a part of the flotilla providing close air support and logistics to the Hook area.

a speedboat shot out from the harbour and not many minutes later, John was seen descending the companionway and climbing aboard the launch. He rejoined us some five days later in Singapore having been flown on ahead in disgrace and critically, without the offending pennant!

Little surprise then when some 15 years later and we had both retired, I phoned his RHQ to ask for his civilian address in Guernsey where I knew he was living and where I was planning to sail. I was puzzled to find no one on the desk seemed to know of him, so I asked to be put through to the Sgt Major. 'No Sir, I am afraid I can't help you – oh, hold on Sir, did you say you are an old friend of his from his Korean War days? Ah, that's different Sir. You see we get so many creditors chasing after him, and seeing as how we like him, we decided the best way to help him was to deny all knowledge. Here's his address.' I think it's called *esprit de corps*.

Let me be clear, John was wholly irrepressible but a very good Troop Leader and friend.

One of the supports we could call on from the front line was air power. We were in contact with planes from the Fleet Air Arm, launching from the British Aircraft carrier HMS *Ocean*, from which the famed Hawker Sea Furys successfully defended our lines from above. As a part of developing the relations between the ground forces and the air support, myself and John Damant were invited on a liaison visit to the carrier to discuss cooperation, meet the people we called up for support from and see how multinational multi-task force combined operations worked in practice.

*Above and below*: The promise of hospitality aboard the HMS *Ocean* was short lived. Our US pilots got lost and took us to the USS *Bairoko* instead. We were given a quick tour of the ship, and then flown back to the mainland.

We flew out to the British carrier in U.S. Navy-piloted Grumman TBM3R Avengers from an airbase in Seoul. Unfortunately, our pilots missed the HMS *Ocean*, and after flying around for a long time, were obliged to land on the USS *Bairoko* instead.

Once safely aboard the US carrier, the ship's awesome scale made it hard to believe we could have completely missed the similarly-sized HMS *Ocean* but as we had approached the *Bairoko* to land it had appeared extremely small, easy to overlook against the massive sea below and far too small for an aircraft to land on safely.

It is still astonishing to me that in the days before GPS and satellite navigation any aircrew ever found any carrier. Fortunately, we didn't stay on board the *Bairoko* long, After Korea she took part in the Bikini Atoll nuclear tests and many of her crew were badly radiated.

On one hand John and I were delighted that we survived the landings and particularly smug that we were on hand to witness the American aircrews getting lost, but our relief turned to horror once onboard the American warship, as did our sympathy for the crew.

While we had been looking forward to the promised 'refreshments' in the wardroom on board the HMS *Ocean*, to our dismay we sadly learnt that American warships were 'dry' – no alcohol was allowed board. We were instead led on a quick tour around the working parts of the carrier by very charming and professional crew members and offered a consoling cup of iced tea, after which we were taken back to the flight deck and catapulted back, sober and hungry, to the mainland.

## R & R to Tokyo

Every soldier sent to Korea was scheduled to spend only one winter there. There was also an obligatory 'Rest and Recuperation' short visit to Japan, (also known as Rack and Ruin) taken while their unit was in reserve. This meant that quite large groups went to Tokyo at any one time.

The journey involved flying in the giant American Globemaster, a Douglas C-124A transport of the 374th Troop Carrier Group. The aircraft was also rather less reverently known as the 'Crashmaster' or 'Old Shaky'. It carried an unprecedented 120 soldiers plus kit and could even carry a number of vehicles which entered the transporter through its nose. The month before I boarded, a C-124 had lost control and crashed in Tokyo and killed all 129 aboard. In 1951 and 1952 107 Cargo aircraft had been destroyed killing 685 personnel. Statistically, going on rest and recuperation to Japan was one of the more dangerous activities in the war!

Fortunately, we arrived safely and Tokyo was an eye opener to any Western visitor. The Japanese recovery from WW2 was astonishing and the shops were full of goods that were still unobtainable in the UK. I bought and sent home a superb dinner service which is still in use nearly 70 years later.

Whilst in Japan I went with three great chums, Desmond, Mickey and Roland, to the small, historic, lakeside town of Nikko which boasted

The Globe Master (or 'Crashmaster' as it was lovingly known) was operated by the United States Air Force and flew a regular 'service' to Japan.

One of the more dangerous parts of the Korean conflict was flying out on R&R. The flights left from an airbase near Seoul, but it wasn't enemy action we were concerned about.

Inside the aircraft there was plenty of space to spread out. You just had to strap everything and everyone down.

beautiful Japanese heritage architecture and where amongst other things, we sampled a fabled Japanese bath in a Geisha House. Out of the front line where Roland did very well, he was never happier than getting away for a few beers. He was everybody's friend. Sadly a few years later he died and alongside the rather formal official obituary detailing his various appointments, was a lovely memory by one of his colleagues which started off, 'Ronald's passing cannot be allowed without the many happy memories of the real Roland we all knew'. It went on, I recall, to say that Roland was never able to appear on the same parade as his Batman as he was always losing his beret, his tie or his puttees and had to borrow them from this devoted but long suffering soldier. Thanks to him, Roland never missed a parade.

Perhaps not the greatest soldier but someone marvellous and memorable to have in the mess and alongside you up at the sharp end when things got tough.

In Tokyo, the call of the Geisha house was irresistible and for sure every soldier experienced at least one while there. What astonished me was

*Above and below*: Tokyo highlighted many differences between East and West. I had a date in Tokyo, and my friends Desmond Bastick and Roland Beard learnt to eat with chopsticks.

Dick Vickers and the padre back in Gloucester valley.

the memory those girls had for our names. (In retrospect this could have resulted in a security breach but no one seemed to care at the time!).

I was in one such house with a group of about five colleagues. Having given the name of our regiment, the girls proceeded to reel off the names of all the other officers who had visited them. One of my colleagues, Desmond, sensed that it might not be best for his promotion prospects if it were known that he too had visited such a place so when they asked his name, he said 'Michael Brown'. The rest of us did a double take knowing full well this was not the name his parents had given him but we played along with the deception. However, his attempt to remain incognito did not go according to plan.

The flimsy geisha house doors suddenly burst open and there stood Roland, a well-known regimental imbiber – swaying slightly. One of the girls asked him if he knew the rest of us and when he replied to the affirmative, they were delighted to demonstrate their skills by reciting all our names 'off pat'. He swayed a bit more visibly when they got to 'Michael Brown' but having completed the roll call, the girls were anxious to add Roland's name to their list. Swaying even more alarmingly, he tried to save himself from toppling over by grabbing on to one of the girls, ripping off her kimono as he fell – accidentally we think – but maybe not! – while identifying himself as Lt Desmond – the real name of Michael Brown!

Not so inebriated after all! Amazingly the girls loved it and for ever after, they told everyone who ever visited the house the story, which grew in the telling, of the robust exploits of poor Lt Desmond of the 1st Tanks. Actually, it did his reputation no harm, in fact rather the opposite, he gained a certain amount of prestige from it and many years later he was promoted to Brigadier! While the geisha girls could outsmart us in most challenges, we won bets by beating them at balancing coins on our bigger noses. It seemed caddish to take advantage of their button noses but British honour was at stake!

Clearly R&R was a great and much-needed break but it also led to broken hearts. One colleague, Mike, fell head-over-heels in love with a strikingly pretty Japanese girl who tearfully bade him a touching farewell at the airport, vowing undying love. Sadly for him, as he was boarding the Globemaster to fly back to Korea, a fault was found in the plane and his flight was delayed. He rushed back inside the Terminal Building expecting to find 'his girl' sobbing into her handkerchief, her face pressed up against the glass, but instead he spied her, far from heart-broken, already focussing her charms on a new arrival.

## The Coronation Parade

Just as the war didn't necessarily take precedence over sport or our weekends, the Commonwealth forces were not going to let the Chinese spoil the celebrations for the Coronation of Queen Elizabeth back in Britain. In the lead up to the Coronation, many senior regiment officers were pulled from the fighting line to prepare for the celebrations and parade. 'A' Sqn even lost its squadron leader – Major S. I. Howard-Jones and 'B' Sqn, in reserve at the time, spent the weeks preparing and painting their tanks for the parade, instead of conducting war-like activities.

At 10 o'clock on June 2nd, Coronation Day, the guns of the Divisional Artillery fired a 'sandwich' of red, white and blue smoke onto the Chinese positions and the RAF flew overhead forming the letters ER in the sky.

Hardly had the smoke started to thin when three salvos of gun fire rang out. On the orders of the Commanding Officer, each tank of the Regiment had fired at a pre-selected target from its battle position.

*Above and right*: For the parade, VIPs flew in by helicopter. R) The South Korean President Syngman Rhee took the salute on a parade featuring thousands of Commonwealth and United Nations soldiers.

The Regimental Headquarters troop led the Commonwealth troops at the Coronation Parade. Despite the war, they had focused on cleaning, servicing and painting the tanks for weeks before the event.

At mid-day, a parade of contingents from all units in the Commonwealth Division was held in the rear areas, attended by Syngman Rhee, the South Korean President, Lt Gen Bruce C. Clark, the United Nations Army Corps Commander and many other high-ranking UN Commanders.

I learned many years later that as a further example of how enthusiastically individual British soldiers supported the event, Lt Bill Nott Bower of the DLI had, the night before, brazenly and very bravely gone over no man's land to lay a display of brightly coloured fluorescent 'Air Recognition Panels' on the Chinese lines. These panels, whose proper use was to pin-point to allied aircraft exactly where the frontline existed, spelt out very visibly and for everyone in the UN lines to see, 'EIIR'. Well done the DLI!

At the coronation parade, a service was given by our Padre, Brian Dougal. Before his tenure with the RTR, he won the Northern Irish Boxing Championship and his fiery sermons invariably had us all cowering in our seats as he listed the horrors that would befall us if we did not listen and comply with his advice – his points being reinforced by an invitation to go three rounds with him if we strayed.

All troops were addressed and congratulated by the UN commander and the Korean President.

A service was given by the Regiment's Padre, Brian Dougal.

Disregarding the Chinese air threat, the RAF flew past in an E for Elizabeth formation.

Following the gun salute, beer was distributed up to the front line for every Commonwealth soldier to celebrate the day. (Photo Denis Croft)

Brian also had the charm of the Irish and there were very few of us who did not consider him to be a valuable, loyal and engaging friend. Immediately after the armistice was sounded, he took a small congregation beyond our frontline wire where amongst the hundreds of Chinese bodies, they met with Chinese soldiers and swapped cigarettes. He eventually wound up as the Deputy Chaplain General of the Army but sadly died at far too young an age.

It was a very symbolic day and we were all proud to play our part. Some 50 years later I was introduced to Prince Philip at a reception at the British Embassy in Oman. I told him of this 'salute by shell fire' on Coronation Day, 1953 and as he moved on, he called back to me over his shoulder, 'Loaded I hope?!'

'Yes Sir! With HE rounds.'

# Chapter 5

# The Battles of the Hook

The Hook was one of the most contested locations of the Korean War since it covered a direct approach to Seoul and was one of the original invasion points used by the North Korean Peoples' Army when they crossed the 38th Parallel in 1950. The 'Hook' was a feature of tactical importance in the Commonwealth divisional sector where the UN Main Line of Resistance (MLR) turned sharply south-west away from the natural line of the Sami-Chon Valley. The Hook gave the occupants the vital high ground advantage covering north and south. The Chinese wanted the position as it gave them an overview of the Imjin River and a perfect place to launch another offensive towards Seoul. Unlike the rest of the Commonwealth line which was about a mile from the Chinese front, the Hook was separated by only 300 yards.

The central ridge of the Hook which gave this precariously-held piece of real estate its name, was around 120 metres above sea level. On the right it was connected to another ridge known as 'Sausage' and on the left rear, to Pt 121. In March 1952 the Hook, held by US Marines, was first contested by the PVA, and Chinese assaults continued throughout the Summer and early Autumn.

Panorama from the forward standing patrol position on the 'Hook'.

A flag presented by the ROK symbolised the trust the South Korean Army held for the UN Forces and in particular our support. We supported a raid they made from our positions at Point 355 'Little Gibraltar'.

## First and Second Battles

On 14th November 1952 the Black Watch, under the command of Lieutenant-Colonel David Rose, relieved the shattered US Marines. They were shocked by the negligent absence of fieldworks and entrenchments and the lack of both any defence in depth or a reserve, factors which jeopardised the line and accounted for heavy and needless US losses. For many months the Chinese had been digging an intricate system of trenches getting ever closer to the American outpost and effectively already shared the northern part of the Hook. Rose, with 800 Korean labourers, a troop of sappers and the Black Watch set about constructing a proper effective defensive position. The Chinese gave the Black Watch four days grace

The frontlines from the Hook, with tank fire impacting the Chinese supporting positions.

before attacking when the new positions were only half-completed. The second battle of the Hook was preceded by a steadily increasing artillery barrage and at about 7pm on 18th November two Companies of Chinese infantry were spotted just below the forward positions on the Hook. Half an hour later the Black Watch company deployed on the Hook was attacked from three different directions.

The Chinese quickly overran the forward positions and the Black Watch was forced back. Rose ordered a counterattack and Centurion tanks from the Skins' and the Black Watch reserve were able to clear the Hook. A few Black Watch soldiers were captured when their forward platoons were overrun but most had stayed safe in their hutchies even though overrun by the Chinese. It was shortly after this action that 1 RTR had taken over as the armoured support and I had spent my first evening on the frontline with the veterans of this battle.

Chinese probing attacks continued throughout the rest of the year and into 1953 and my spells on the front line were spent wondering if tonight would be the night the Chinese 'kicked off' again. It was partly to dissuade these attacks and partly because the PVA were applying more pressure on this part of the line that motivated me to fire off more rounds than any other

Trooper Devine keeps watch over the Chinese positions at the Hook.

troop in the squadron. However, the prospect certainly kept us on our toes. We were relieved by American troops in February and we took our tanks off the line with the rest of the Commonwealth Division to rest, reorganise and retrain.

Among the many precedents that the Regiment claims to have set whilst in Korea was a unique working arrangement with American tanks. 'A' Squadron was the first to establish this relationship and trained American tank crews to direct shoots for them. This also worked very successfully in reverse when 'A' Squadron directed American tanks on to targets that they were unable to see. It is thought that this was the first occasion where unilateral fire orders have been employed.

We relieved the Americans and returned to our original positions on the front in April when the valley around the Hook had exploded into the colours of spring and the fields were alive with wild flowers.

'C' Squadron, now in the Hook area, created another precedent with an interesting technique for killing the Chinese at night. At that time the tanks were not equipped with night vision optics, but the Infantry used Infra-Red scopes. When they observed the enemy infantry at certain pre-designated points, they informed the tanks, who were able to engage these pre-registered coordinates blind.

A Korean Division was supported in a raid by a troop of 'B' Squadron in the area of hill 355. They engaged enemy machine gun posts and their communication trenches to prevent the arrival of enemy reinforcements whilst the raid was taking place. Later, during an enemy night attack on the Canadian Brigade, another troop from 'B' Squadron had been engaging enemy gun flashes and communication trenches and received heavy concentrations of enemy fire in return. That the enemy never embarked upon an operation without engaging our tanks first was, we all felt, flattering, if uncomfortable.

With the advent of the hot dry weather, activity on all parts of the front increased considerably, both from the point of view of patrolling and shelling. A two-company PVA attack on the night of 2nd May against the 3rd Bn Royal Canadian Regiment, managed to overrun a forward platoon position but it was restored by first light by a counterattack launched by the reserve company with tanks from 'B' Squadron. They had been supporting the Canadians by engaging enemy gun flashes and received heavy harassing fire in return from enemy 122mm guns.

## The Third Battle

The third battle for the Hook started on 7th May with a heavy daylight bombardment of the Black Watch positions and a reported build-up of Chinese infantry in the caves at the foot of its hill. After an hour of artillery shelling and supporting fire from 3 Troop, the Chinese appeared to have abandoned their attack but they tried again at 2am. The Chinese approach was detected by the Black Watch's standing patrols which triggered a second defensive barrage and spirited defence. The Duke of Wellington's Regiment relieved the Black Watch on the night of 12/13th May with the expectation of being attacked at any time.

Chinese loud speakers boasted that the British would be evicted from the Hook on the 13th. We quickly briefed the Dukes on the lay of the land along with the positions of the minefields and our tank DF plans and made sure every company commander in the Hook defences had a map with an overlaying trace of the pre-arranged tasks. The Dukes also had two troops of Centurions from 'C' Squadron in support.

The author on the Hook with 'Mersa Mutruh'.

B Squadron officers compare experiences before the debrief starts.

The Chinese returned to the Hook on the night of 17/18th May shortly after 11pm when the Dukes' standing patrols heard the Chinese chattering and saw movement across all the spurs leading into the Hook. As the Chinese approached, artillery and tank fire were called down and the patrols opened fire with their own weapons. A prisoner captured in the early morning of 18th May gave invaluable warning of an impending Chinese attack, although not the exact date of the attack. The Chinese would outnumber the defenders by almost five to one and their method of approach would guarantee them relative immunity from the existing planned concentrations of artillery fire. This new information gave us time to reschedule our DF plans and re-site the defences.

On 28th May, at about 10.15am the Chinese mortaring and shelling began again and would not stop until the battle was over. After a horrendous three-minute bombardment, the Chinese rushed the Hook and two minutes later, they were on top of the forward positions.

At 8.45pm, the Chinese launched a second wave of fresh troops and although they were badly savaged by artillery, tank and machine-gun fire, they succeeded in joining the survivors of the first attack on the forward positions. Fierce hand to hand combat ensued around the forward trenches with the Centurions using their close range 2-inch mortars to help repel the enemy.

Colonel Gerry debriefed the Regiment after the 3rd Hook battle. I was told that 3 Troop had fired by far the most rounds of any troop in the regiment and was awarded a bow and arrow set by Arthur Thrift.

Elsewhere on the Hook, two fresh companies of Chinese attacked Pt 121 but were caught in a ferocious concentration of artillery, tank and machine-gun fire and suffered the most appalling casualties. Only six of them got as far as the wire in front of the trenches and their attack crumbled. The Chinese switched their attention to Pt 146 where two companies from the King's Regiment waited for them. For the second time that night, the artillery shredded the Chinese as they formed up. It was learned later a complete Chinese battalion had been caught by the guns and virtually wiped out.

The last wave of this attack on the Hook was launched at 12.30am on 29th May and beaten off. At dawn on 30th May, the full extent of the devastation on the Hook was revealed. Ten thousand Chinese shells had ploughed into the hill and levelled it like a well-worn football pitch. Chinese casualties could only be estimated at around 250 dead and 800 wounded. The Dukes suffered 149 casualties of whom 28 were killed and 16 men were taken prisoner. During the third Battle of the Hook, more than 37,000 British shells, 10,000 mortar bombs and half a million rounds of small arms ammunition were fired. For seven hours, one American gun fired an illuminating flare every two minutes.

Although no attacks were launched at 'B' Squadron on the right, the entire front received considerable suppressing fire from enemy guns and mortars; Point 159 where I was, again taking the brunt and one tank

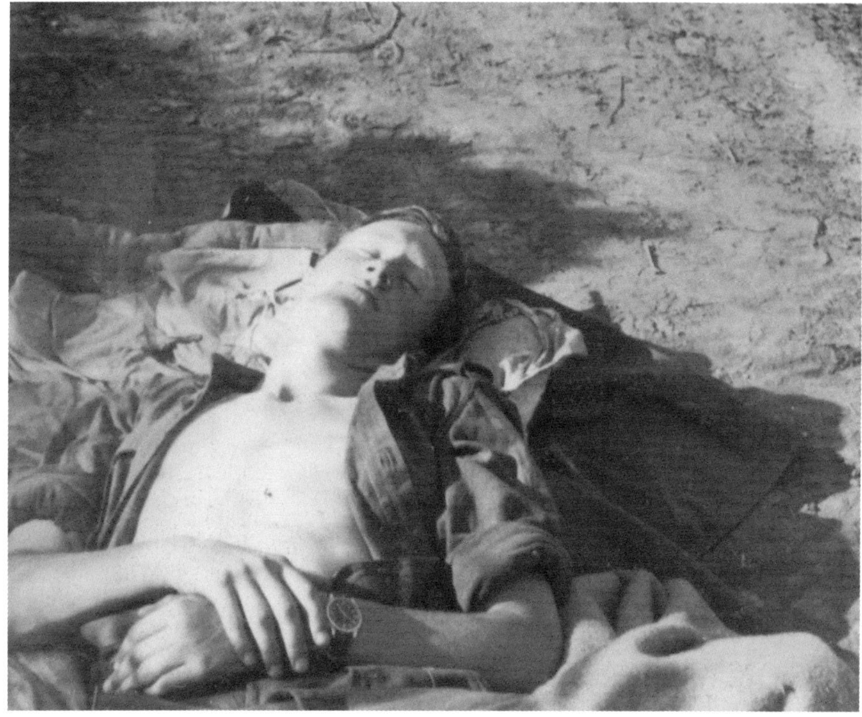

3 Troop moved to the hook at the end of May to support the Royal Fusiliers in a possible counter attack on the threatened Hook salient held by the Dukes. We weren't needed but we had many sleepless nights braced for impact and on full alert. The order to stand down came after a number of days without sleep. I was caught napping by a crew member who borrowed my camera!

received a direct hit from an 85 mm AP shot which made a deep gouge on the nose plate but failed to penetrate.

## The Fourth Battle

I was promoted in early July and was now working directly for Dick Ward as his Battle Captain at Squadron HQ. This was a cherished role, especially since promotion opportunities within such a highly experienced regiment were limited and many subalterns were frustratingly held back from promotion by the surfeit of over-qualified veterans in reduced roles. At any other time, Arthur Thrift and Dick Ward would have been commanding a brigade, but here they were running a squadron. My role was now to assist

The view of the Chinese positions from the Hook.

and shadow the Squadron Leader and be prepared to take over should he be incapacitated or killed. Jack Dutton, an exchange officer from the Special Service Battalion of the South African Army (and later to be a senior general) took over 'my' 3 Troop.

With the peace talks in Panmunjom reaching a conclusion, the Chinese were eager to gain a last-minute propaganda victory over the UN Forces and their final assault on the Hook was the last of the war before the official signing of the Truce applied the terms of the Armistice.

The fourth Battle of the Hook, also known as The Battle of the Samichon River, lasted two days and resulted in the defending UN troops, including 2 RAR from the Brigade and a US Marines unit, repulsing numerous assaults over 24/26 July. There were also two concerted night attacks which

In the Squadron HQ, Squadron Leader Dick Ward and the 'Battle Captain' discuss the dispositions.

inflicted numerous casualties on the PVA due to our heavy artillery, tank and small-arms fire.

During the last two nights of the war 'B' Squadron came in for a lot of shelling during attacks on adjacent American positions. The two left-hand troops from their positions were able to engage the attacking enemy and were in action continuously during both nights, killing a considerable number of enemy and assisting materially in the successful defence of the positions.

John Nolan, a crewman in 3 Troop, had an eventful night. He was deployed in a 3 Troop Centurion on a feature on the Hook known as the 'Sausage'. His account of the action follows:

> *On the evening of the 23rd Sgt Marsh and Percy went on Stag. It was their task to take the tank's medicine chest with them. It contained various wound dressings, powders, oiled dressing for burns and more importantly, morphine ampoules. Unfortunately, that night, they forgot.*

*Once in the tank there were two lines of communication to the outside; a phone box at the rear of the tank for infantry cooperation and to advise those on stag, that the next stag wanted entry. There was also a telephone land line laid from the tank which was mainly used to wake up the sleeping crews in the hoochie for the change of stag and was rung loudly and repeatedly. This could also be used to alert nearby infantry that something was happening on the Chinese positions or in no man's land.*

*That night I'd woken early. It was always difficult to sleep before midnight. One normally dropped off about 2100 to 2200 hrs but being woken from a deep sleep was hard to take.*

*I'd made my way to the tank at about 2340 hrs, used the phone to gain entry and was then given a sitrep by Geoff Marsh on what had occurred, what might occur and the*

John Nolan (3rd from left) would later transfer to the Australian Army and become Squadron Sergeant major of 'A' Squadron Australian SAS Regiment. From left, the remainder are Cpl Ross Thompson RNZAC, Pete Stubbs and Bill Rudram. Ross and Bill replaced Sgt Doug Marsh and L/Cpl Percy who were WIA during a blue on blue artillery strike on 23rd July at the Fourth Hook.

*possibility of a Chinese attack against the left flank of The Hook and the right flank of the US 1st Marine Division. If this attack occurred, then a counter barrage would be put down right across The Hook and Hills 108 and 110. We would be advised of this barrage by a code word which he was about to tell me, when Squadron HQ came on the net with a call sign 42 'Bull shit now'.*

*As I relayed this message to Geoff, there was a loud bang and the commander's cupola hatch shot open. Because the Chinese were so close, our own artillery was firing on our position and a 'blue on blue' high explosive 25 pounder airburst, one of many, had burst immediately above the tank. The hatch was unlocked and open in readiness for the next crew change and the turret filled with cordite and some shrapnel. Geoff and Percy were both hit. Geoff's wound was a deep penetration of his chest and Percy had been hit in the groin.*

*I made the necessary wireless report, something I will always remember: 'Hello 42 easy for 42, my number one and number three have been yoked, I say again, my number one and number three have been yoked, request "Starlight"'. (Starlight was the Armoured Ambulance Recovery Vehicle).*

*Geoff was moaning, more concerned that his pregnant wife would be informed, while Percy was emotionally strained and trying to see where he had been hit and what he might have lost.*

*I couldn't find the first aid box and realising it was probably still in the bunker, I tried to call Pete Stubbs to ask him to bring it with him but the line had been cut during the bombardment. So, I had to venture out, make my way through the barrage to the bunker where I found Pete fast asleep. Here I also located the box.*

*Having woken my mucker, I then made my way back to our tank. The whole of The Hook was lit up, the counter barrage progressing back again. I tried the tank phone but it didn't work, the wiring was cut in several places. So, I stood on*

> *the side of the tank, now lit up like a Xmas tree and tried to attract their attention by hammering on the steel of the hatch, as I knew they were still conscious. But they thought that my hammering was the Chinese, trying to gain entry. Finally, they let me in. I dressed Doug's wound first with an oiled dressing, then two wound dressings.*
>
> *I'd given him a cigarette and saw the smoke curling out of the wound. He was still more concerned about his wife. Percy meanwhile had calmed down and had dressed his own wound, so we waited for the Squadron's ambulance tug to arrive.*
>
> *Pete Stubbs had by then joined us and when the tug arrived, helped assist Doug out of the tank, while Percy made his own way to the tug.*
>
> *After this we then both settled down back into the tank, Pete as commander/gunner, while I acted as loader operator, and continued to fire the 20-pounder main gun and 7.62mm coax Best on any infantry approved fixed targets, before lobbing 2" high explosive and phosphorus shells in front of the tank at the enemy, who at most were only 50 yds away. (I recall that before long we had fired off most of our supply as we were faced with having to physically replenish the next day, both the main armament ammunition as well as the coax and 2" mortars.*

2 Tp now under Jack Dutton had a tough night in the battle and listening in on the radio at Squadron HQ, I had to be constrained by Dick Ward from leaping into a Jeep and going up front to support them!

I had spent the two days at SHQ, obviously disappointed to miss the action but busy as hell supporting the squadron and monitoring the battle's progress. The PVA attempted to breakthrough to the Imjin by exploiting any weak points between the US and the Commonwealth Divisions, so my key task was ensuring that any vulnerabilities were covered and the Regiment's mobile reserves were prepared to counter any Chinese gains.

However, the front lines held and the reserve would not be called for. Well-coordinated fire from the divisional artillery and support from the entrenched infantry helped 2 RAR successfully thwart both assaults and

Jack Dutton, here standing with the Hook behind, was given command of 3 Troop for the final Battle.

NZ Gunners visited the troop after the truce.

hold onto the Hook. UN sources estimated PVA casualties at 2,000 to 3,000 killed; the majority of them inflicted by Kiwi gunners.

It is impossible to recall 'the Hook' without taking one's hat off to the incredible role played by the Artillery. I think that, unquestionably, without their support the Chinese would have taken the Hook that night and many Commonwealth lives.

The artillery used something called a VT (Variable Timing) fuse which allowed the shell to be set to explode about 6 or 8 feet above ground and the damage the shell splinters and shrapnel did to the human waves of infantry

Major Ward and the author on a visit to B Squadron positions on the Hook.

the Chinese flung at the defences was indescribable. In one of the battles, they fired over 15,000 shells, a number equalled only at the famous Battle of El Alamein in WW2 – yet Korea, where the fighting was just as brutal, is a forgotten war.

This tribute to the Gunners in no way diminishes the superhuman achievements of the different British and Australian infantry battalions. On at least three attempts by the Chinese to secure this strategically important feature dominating the route to Seoul, they held off massive, determined Chinese attempts to capture it while the Truce negotiations proceeded. We all knew the outcome would determine the permanent frontier between North and South Korea after the Truce was declared, and the propaganda value of a Chinese success.

Britain and the world should be forever proud of those infantry men and their achievements. These guys fought with dogged courage and determination possibly equalled but never bettered in all our long history.

I would like to recall the comment made by the Brigade Commander about the Duke of Wellington's who he had tasked to hold the Hook in

Major Ward read out the terms of the Truce to the Squadron.

one battle. After this fearsome fight with the Chinese crawling all over the feature but failing to dislodge the Dukes, the Brigadier commented the next morning, 'Everything depended on the Dukes holding the feature and they did as I knew they would'.

What a wonderfully inspirational group of men they were. It was an honour to have supported them and the other battalions on the Hook in every way we could. But I am sure these gallant men, with all their bravery and skills, would agree they could not have competed with the waves of thousands of Chinese set at them, had these hordes not been significantly decimated by the Gunners before they got there. The last battle for the Hook had been as violent as any part of the war, even though it was waged hours before everyone on both sides knew the war would end and further bloodshed was needless.

Only a few hours later, the armistice agreement was signed, ultimately ending the war. Both sides were subsequently obliged to withdraw 2 kilometres within 72 hours to create the 4 kilometre Demilitarised Zone that still defines the border between North and South Koreas. A Chinese success at the Hook might have seen Chinese forces across the Imjin and in a far stronger position. This might have jeopardised the proposed armistice terms and endangered Seoul's, and hence South Korea's, future.

# Chapter 6

# The Truce

Whatever was happening during the prolonged Truce talks, which had dragged on for years, there was no indication on the front line that the Chinese aggression would let up. However, the threat of a ceasefire freezing the current battle lines without any Chinese domination had prompted them to make a final attack for purely PR gains.

This fruitless final assault had left us in little doubt that the Chinese could not be trusted to honour a truce when it came, so after the ceasefire came into effect at 2200hrs on the 27th July 1953, the UN retained a defensive war footing. Both sides were obliged to withdraw 2 kilometres

The stench of dead Chinese was appalling. The PVA were generally pretty good about collecting their dead and wounded but after the Hook assaults, most were left where they fell. Major Ward brought the squadron down to no man's land to see the aftermath before moving back to establish new positions.

Once the signal for the Truce was sounded at 10am, both sides emerged from cover to survey the valley floor. It wasn't a pretty sight. John Nolan recalls the smell: the slow thick black green decomposing odour down the side of the main trench on The Hook: the residue of two opposed frontal attacks of December and January, (met by the Black Watch) and from May and June (met by The Dukes). This mulch of Chinese bodies covered the approach of the last, futile Chinese attack. This was carried out across open ground, in broad daylight and into the barrages of both their own covering screen and the massed UN artillery.

from their front lines within 72 hours to create the 4 kilometre Demilitarised Zone but several surprises were in store. The first was that the moment the ceasefire was sounded a number of Chinese soldiers emerged out of the ground next to our front line positions. They had presumably moved into these positions at night and buried themselves in by our wire. They were yards away from our defences and would have reached us in seconds if the conflict had continued. At the signal of the truce, they emerged from the ground, looked at us and wandered back to the Chinese lines without saying a word.

The other surprise, given the tight schedule for evacuating the demilitarised zone, was that Dick Ward took the whole squadron on foot over no man's land. Right up against our barbed wire defences lay mounds of dead Chinese soldiers. I think he was anxious that plenty of witnesses

1 RTR's officers mess in Gloucester Valley.

could confirm that the United Nations had had the upper hand. Certainly there were hundreds, if not thousands, of bodies. The stench of decay was appalling but it showed without any doubt that in spite of the heroic defence by the infantry who gave not one inch, the tide was turned by the dedicated success of the Artillery and their incredibly brave and skilful forward observation officers. Heroes all.

## New Defensive Positions

We were given three days to clear the battlefield of military equipment and destroy our defences, before moving back and leaving a demilitarised zone. We effectively became a labour battalion and the next three days were some of the hardest that the Regiment had had since its arrival in Korea, as there was a vast amount of material to be uprooted and moved. However, the job was completed and the tanks, battered yet indomitable, rolled back from the frontlines. The Regiment found itself once more together in Gloucester Valley with a new role preparing a new defensive line, codenamed 'Kansas', in case the Chinese broke the Truce.

We moved the tanks back from the front line to create the demilitarised zone and fulfil the truce's conditions.

We were tasked to develop a secure line around Pintail Bridge, a crossing point of the Imjin River which required new emplacements and shelters. We had support from sappers but the bulk of the work was manual and an opportunity for the tank crews to spend time in the sun without worrying about incoming artillery.

Heavy rains and heat made the new fortified line a challenging task.

The camp site at Gloucester Valley. A semi-permanent base and new defensive line (codenamed Kansas) in case the Chinese tried it on again.

We worked harder in the weeks following the truce than at any other time in Korea, partly because we didn't trust the Chinese to keep the truce and partly because it rained heavily while we were preparing our defensive positions.

We also had to erect permanent accommodation in Gloucester Valley for the troops who would police the new border and this included the construction of hundreds of Quonset huts (the American version of the British Nissen Hut) which we distributed and erected. These lightweight prefabricated structures were made of corrugated galvanised steel with a semi-cylindrical cross-section and my troop spent weeks distributing them.

One camp was located next to a Yankee Infantry battalion who proudly displayed a sign saying 'XYZ Infantry Battalion – Second to None'. A few hundred yards down the road a British battalion had stuck up an even larger notice displaying their name as 'ABC Battalion – None'.

At the end of September, the Regiment had the melancholy task of saying goodbye to Colonel G. C. Hopkinson who was returning to England en route to take command of 33 Armoured Brigade in Germany. To him the Regiment owes a very great debt of gratitude, for he above all others was responsible for the Regiment's great success in Korea. He handed over temporary command to Major H. P. S. Massey and it wasn't until the end

of November that we were able to welcome our new commanding officer, Colonel N.E O. Watts, who was flown from England to arrive just in time to take command before the Regiment left Korea. Fortunately, he arrived in time to command the Regiment at the Farewell Parade which was attended by the new GOC Major General H. Murray and all the senior officers of the Commonwealth Division. The parade was followed by a lunch party at which over 150 guests were present.

*Above, below and opposite above*: The new Officers' Mess was designed by Captain Peter Wilson and built largely by the officers. Alan Parks, Peter Davis and Martin Sinett try it out for size.

To the soldiers' delight the Officers' Mess burnt down shortly after construction. The probable culprit, a candle.

Towards the end of November, during a particularly cold spell, a five day exercise was carried out, during which the new defence line was occupied and defended against powerful hostile attacks which the directing staff conjured up at all hours of the day and night.

I was responsible for distributing the Quonset huts.

RTR Officers outside the new squadron offices.

In the last few weeks, I ran a tank commanders' course.

*Above and overleaf spread*: The RTR organised a Divisional Athletics Championship in the last months before leaving Korea. Team sports were organised daily and there was time to go swimming in local streams, hunt for souvenirs and even join organised shoots for duck and pheasant. We also started to think about and train for our next posting – the Suez canal.

Following the truce and the mad rush to prepare the base and new defensive lines, our attention turned to staving off boredom. The Chinese seemed unlikely to push their luck and at that stage we weren't worried that North Korea would try anything foolish either. We transitioned from a war footing to an occupation force that frankly didn't want to be there. Boredom became the enemy but we met it head on with exercises, training courses, sports and social events. We held an athletics tournament for the Commonwealth Division before preparing to leave Korea.

## Our Departure

It was not long before the Regiment started to get ready to depart Korea. It would be handing over to our sister regiment, 5 RTR and the Regiment would leave Korea on 15 December. I was selected to be on the advance

As a part of the advance party to Suez, I travelled from Pusan to Japan again (but separately from the Regiment). I had another few days leave there and then headed back to Pusan.

The United Nations Cemetery in Pusan.

party to prepare for the move to the Canal Zone in Egypt where once again we were to take over from the Skins.

We were flown again to Kure in Japan and after a short bonus R&R break, we boarded the P&O Troopship – the luxurious *Asturias* which returned us to Pusan to pick up and travel with the Duke of Wellingtons' main body before sailing on to Egypt.

Ashore in Pusan, we attended a most moving memorial service in the British War Cemetery. Astonishingly, after five months in permanent

We attended the United Nations cemetery in Pusan and paid our respects to Trooper Dixon, the only member of 1 RTR to lose his life in the conflict and to my friend Johnny Tresawna, of the Oxfordshire and Buckinghamshire Light Infantry who was killed in June whilst serving with the DLI. Trooper Dixon had been travelling to the rear from the front line in a scout car and was caught by artillery.

The Turkish cemetery was significantly larger and gave us an opportunity to reflect on and appreciate our superior leadership, equipment and training.

The band saw us off with similar tunes to our arrival, and the same lack of military authority!

Pusan, 13th November 1953, aboard the HMT *Asturias* and leaving Korea for the final time.

My final view of Korea, sadly I have never returned.

contact with the enemy, the Regiment had lost only one soldier killed. It was a testament to our squadrons' leadership and the design of the Centurion. Also attending this service were the Dukes who would have to leave 60 of their comrades interred in Korea. It was an honour to be surrounded by so many brave men.

PART TWO

# ...TO THE GREEN FIELDS BEYOND

## Serving with the Royal Tank Regiment 1953–1960

# Chapter 7

# Soldiering On

## The Canal Zone

I arrived back in Suez aboard the *Asturias* by early December 1953 for a short posting. I was part of the Regiment's advance element and arrived a few weeks before the main body of the regiment to prepare to take over from the Skins for the second time in a year. We were stationed in Shandur, a purpose built camp beside the Little Bitter Lake, part of the Suez Canal.

All shipping passed up and down the canal in convoys – one in the morning and one in the evening, and these convoys would pass each other

RTR members watched the French troops passing through the canal on the way to Vietnam. The ships had armed sentries prepared to shoot any of their own men that tried to jump ship.

We patrolled many villages, looking for stolen equipment, stores and fuel.

RTR members preparing to go out on patrol along the Canal. After Korea, it was difficult to deal with the resentment that many of the locals felt towards the British. We also didn't appreciate that the locals saw theft from us as an act of resistance, as much as a source of personal enrichment.

*Above and below*: We patrolled the zone in modified Land Rovers and were armed to the teeth. It was hard not to think of the LRDG or SAS as we sped though the desert. These were a welcome diversion from the Centurions which offered the crews little observation.

in the wide expanses of the Bitter Lakes. We could watch them at close hand and I particularly remember French troopships taking soldiers to the War in Vietnam. This was already an unpopular war, particularly with French conscripts, and it was a sad reflection to see armed guards posted along the ships' sides ready to shoot any of their own soldiers who jumped overboard hoping to escape what was clearly going to be an arduous posting.

From the base at Shandur, our role was to guard the canal and its installations to ensure that ships could move freely and to protect the regional assets, such as power stations, from sabotage attack by Egyptian resistance fighters objecting to British control. This included protecting the 'sweet water canal' which ran parallel to the main canal, providing freshwater to the villages and army bases along the banks.

Three years before the Suez crisis, tensions were already high and there was a great deal of pilfering, with Egyptians cutting through the camp wire and stealing anything they could lay their hands on, from full petrol cans

The 'Korean' Bell was made from empty tank shell cases in a Korean foundry from brass collected from our Centurions' position. I like to think that I contributed to its construction. It was completed in time for our Suez deployment and unveiled in Shandhur. It is now rung every year at a regimental parade on Korea Day.

Major Ward commanded the Squadron in Shandhur.

Training and patrolling in the desert for a number of scenarios.

The desert offered fantastic manoeuvre training after the static lines in Korea.

to food from the cook houses. This was a real threat and required constant patrolling of the boundary wire at night. It was a 'jumpy' duty for the soldiers. How easily your imagination saw a creeping shadow and attacked it only to find it was a bush.

The Regiment was back and operating in the same region where it had excelled during the Second World War. We were equipped with Centurions, again handed over from the Skins, and worked with many different units, this time preparing and training for a potentially mobile war.

In one scenario, the Regiment worked with the Parachute Regiment and had a contingency plan prepared to support them in operations against the capital city, Cairo. Most of the training was routine and after the thrills of Korea, some soldiers needed ways to add extra colour to the posting, one soldier in particular ending in very hot water.

When not on patrol, there was time to relax on the beaches.

1 RTR back to its roots, in the perfect tank environment of the desert.

*Above and below*: The Officers' Mess and the Sailing Club at Shandhur. Swimming in the Red Sea at the weekends.

The garden of the Officers' Mess in Shandhur overlooked the sailing club and canal.

One of those memorable 'salt of the earth' type soldiers who was always in trouble 'without it being his fault' ended up in an Egyptian cell where he was awaiting his next Court Martial. As we talked, he made it very clear that he did not agree with the sentence he had just received. He blamed it on an ineffective defence by his counsel, Lieutenant XY. When I asked him, as was expected of me, and as was his right, who he would like to defend him this time, he pondered for a while and then answered 'Sir, could we change the rules. Could I ask that Lieutenant XY be appointed to "prosecute me"'?

For sure it was an interesting sally but also a telling point and indeed, I sympathised with him. I do recall with pleasure that the officer I suggested should defend him succeeded and he became a free man again!!

There was another soldier who was always in trouble but again, always blameless! I had sent a letter to the parents of all soldiers in my unit reporting on the year's activities and received a delightful reply from this particular soldier's mother thanking me for helping improve her son's education.

1RTR Officers in tropical uniforms at Shanhur. Yet again I was on leave when this was taken.

Slightly surprised at this misplaced gratitude, I sought to discover the source of this misinterpretation. It turned out that the naughty boy had told his mother that the 'M.C.E', that appeared embossed on his homeward mail, in which he had spent several 'attachments', stood for Military College of Education, whereas in reality, it stood for Military Corrective Establishment!

Battle exercises were conducted by the tanks in the desert and as I was now second in command of the squadron, my role was to ensure there was sufficient fuel, ammunition and supplies for the tanks and that all the crews got their meals.

The role also involved coordinating movement and tactics with the squadron leader and assuming his role when he was away. I enjoyed this aspect of soldiering but in March I was sent on leave with orders to report to the UK. I travelled back to Britain by ship from Port Said to Athens and then boat hopped and trained across Europe as part of my leave. When I arrived in Britain I visited AG 17 at the War Office in Stanmore to discuss my next posting. Here I was offered a choice of three jobs and happily accepted the plum job of Staff Captain at 23 Armoured Brigade TA Headquarters based in Chester under command of the famed Desert Warrior, Brigadier Bill Liardet.

Like the *Halladale*, the troopship *Asturias* ferried troops from Korea to Britain throughout the conflict and to the Eastern outposts of the empire until the early 1960s when troops were flown.

*Left and below*: Troop ships from Britain and France passed through the canal to get to Korea, Hong Kong and Vietnam.

We were horrified to learn that the French troopships heading out to Vietnam posted armed guards with instructions to shoot French soldiers who might try to desert by jumping ship in the narrow canal. We would never have imagined taking such drastic action and could only image how low morale must have been aboard. On the way out to Korea, even our conscripted soldiers had been keen to 'get stuck in'.

However, there was time to fish in the canal.

*Above and below*: The Regiment was significantly understrength following the demobilisation of its national servicemen. In addition to meeting the military obligations of a full complement, 1 RTR was also expected to improve the camp security as the Muslim Brotherhood ramped up its insurgency.

*Above and below*: We spent a lot of our spare-time preparing the dinghies for races.

## Two Glorious Years in the UK

No wonder I was called 'Lucky Jim'. Proudly displaying my new Korean War ribbons and driving a brand new Morris Minor, I drove from Mill Hill where my father lived, to the depot of the Cheshire Regiment in the Dale just north of Chester. Within this depot, occupying a large hut, was located the Headquarters of 23 Armoured Brigade TA, my home for the next two years.

Considering our responsibilities, we were a small team consisting of the Brigadier, Bill Liardet CB, CBE, DSO, formerly of the Royal Tank Regiment, the Brigade Major, Geoff Blundell-Brown, a charismatic 'Skin', perfectly made for the role, combining the skills needed to be highly effective and the charm to get his way, and myself as Staff Captain with the Bond-esque title 'Q'. Later Brigadier Joe Fishbourne, (a former Skin who had also fought in Korea) took over from Bill Liardet.

Within the Brigade were some remarkable territorial army regiments such as the Cheshire Yeomanry, the Shropshire Yeomanry, the North Staffordshire Yeomanry, the 40th (Kings) Royal Tank Regiment of Liverpool and the Liverpool Scottish. All these regiments were commanded by distinguished

On exercise in Germany, the Brass visited us to monitor our exercises. Budgets and cutbacks were beginning to take a hold, not that you'd guess it from their waistlines!

Family and Friends Day at Bovington Camp and the Tank Museum.

The author at a visit from an RTR General.

Second World War commanders and it was invigorating to work with such people who were not only great soldiers but also successful businessmen.

Administratively speaking, the highlight of my two years in Cheshire was organising and implementing the 1955 biannual brigade exercises on

Salisbury Plain. Duties involved planning the accommodation and food, marshalling the required number of tanks and other vehicles and, perhaps most interesting of all, going to British Rail Headquarters at Euston to organise the five or six special trains needed to get the different regiments in the Brigade to the local railheads.

It was fashionable to decry British Rail at that time too, but one spring day I sat in a large room at Euston Station with representatives of probably 10 different regions where the conversation ran something like this: 'I can take over Military Special at Crewe at 09.47 and deliver it at Birmingham at 10.42.' Then another guy would say 'I can collect it at 10.48 and deliver it to Bristol at 12.18'. The master controller would interrupt saying 'what happens if Goods Train G54 delays it?' and immediately these extraordinary controllers would give the standby solutions. It is presumably done by computer now but gosh it was impressive and I never criticised British Rail again!

The TA soldiers were every bit as keen on professionalism as were their regular army opposite numbers. Attending occasional 'drill nights', I was full of admiration for these guys and their desire and ability to perform every bit as well as their regular counterparts. Their enthusiasm was contagious and I hope it is not patronising to say that while such people exist, Britain has little to fear.

Before travelling to Cheshire, I had had little thought for the social impact of my appointment. However, I hadn't been in Chester long before I realised the locals not only had the warmth of their more northern colleagues but also enough money to be enormously generous in their hospitality.

Then there were also glamorous sporting and cultural events such as the Grand National at Aintree and numerous hunter trials. We also attended the Welsh Eisteddfod, performances in Liverpool by leading companies such as Covent Garden Opera and Ballet, major Symphony orchestras and pre-West End theatre productions. One highlight was motor racing at Oulton Park and I remember watching with admiration the skills of Stirling Moss competing against Mike Hawthorn and being very amused to hear what they got up to at the all-night party afterwards. I had taken a stunning girl to the event but had had to leave while the party was still in full swing as I had early morning military duties. When I asked her how she got home, she replied 'I was driven home by Stirling Moss but I'm not sure who was fastest, Stirling Moss driving or Mike Hawthorn in the back with me'!

*Above and below*: Fire power display on the ranges at Lulworth Cove.

The Dale Depot Cheshire Regiment Officers' Mess had two tennis courts which meant we could return some of the hospitality we received by holding tennis parties every Thursday throughout the summer. There was no shortage of partners and before long, my car was joining the queue waiting outside "the local secretarial college" in Chester just as the girls were putting the covers on their typewriters at the end of the day. It was fun sweeping away from the kerb with your girl before your colleagues could identify her and rag you mercilessly thereafter.

It was in Chester that I took over a black Labrador puppy named Kiwi, after the black shoe polish. She will appear frequently in the following pages of my story. A remarkable loving companion for over 15 years, she well and truly earned her place in my heart.

Also in Chester we had a very close brush with the law. My Army boss had been out on an early morning shoot and in a fit of enthusiasm, shot a swan which is of course illegal, the swans being a protected species and closely connected to the Queen. Guilt overtook him and he passed the bird to me with instructions for it to be quickly transformed into a pie to be served up at dinner in the Mess. The Mess Manager was made of sterner stuff and said that she would have no part in this incident and returned the carcass to me. Meanwhile one of the Mess staff had informed the police who came out to follow up on this report. Luckily, I had secreted the poor bird in the boot of my car and after the police had inspected the Mess, I came out onto the doorstep to wish them goodbye only to spot to my horror out of the corner of my eye, my faithful Labrador sitting drooling behind the car, her nose pressed against the boot. To my great relief, the police shot away in a spray of gravel with barely a backward glance.

Altogether it was the most amazing two year experience, as could be seen from the entries in my diary which showed only two nights during the whole of my last six weeks in post without an invitation to some civilian or military social event.

It was with a heavy heart that I bought an export-priced Hillman Minx Convertible and drove off to my next posting in Berlin as 2 i/c of the Independent Squadron of the Royal Tank Regiment.

## Berlin 1956-1957

The 1st (Berlin) Independent Squadron, RTR was formed in November 1951 under Major Rollo Cambell during the Berlin Blockade, to provide armoured support to the British Independent Infantry brigade there. Having personally been responsible for holding back the hordes of Chinese infantry that threatened the Korean Peninsula, I was confident that our 16 obsolete World War Two Comet tanks could hold off the Russian army should they dare to try to invade the British Zone of Berlin! Officially, the Squadron's task was to wave a flag to encourage West Berliners to believe that we were sincere in protecting their interest, and it was to be a very interesting, valuable and fun posting. We were stationed in Spandau Barracks next to Spandau prison in which the last of the Nazi war criminals were held. The British, French, American and Russian forces took it in turns to guard the prisoners and it was interesting to see that when it was the turn of the Russians, the British made sure they were routed past the glamorous shops in the wealthiest areas of Berlin, just to give them an idea of what they were missing as Communists.

We trained seriously in Berlin and I attended many joint exercises with the local infantry in the Grunewald Forest. On one such exercise, I was rather proud to note that one of my leading tanks came up on the radio to report that the 'enemy' had overrun a platoon position. I passed this on to Brigade HQ who came back 10 minutes later rather rudely denying it. 'Hmm', I thought. I rechecked and had it confirmed. Probably an hour or so later, Brigade reported that the platoon was indeed overrun. From then on I always discussed radio communications with any infantry I was supporting and I am rather proud to say that our swift communications were always treated as 'gospel'.

The Queen's Birthday Parade in Berlin, starting from the Olympic Stadium.

This Dingo armoured car finished the exercise early.

For larger exercises, we were taken by train to the British Zone in West Germany. Berlin was deep inside the Soviet Zone of Germany and access to the city was heavily controlled. All movement was also controlled by the Soviets. The Berliner train from Charlottenburg in West Berlin to Braunschweig in the British Zone of West Germany ran every day, apart from Christmas Day and during the Berlin Blockade. Those driving from the British Zone could only cross at Checkpoint Alpha, the Helmstedt-Marienborn crossing, and the journey between Berlin and West Germany had to follow a set route and be completed in a set time. Whilst in Berlin as 2 i/c of the Squadron I was in charge of a programme known as Current Affairs, designed to see that everyone knew what was going on and why we were or could be involved. For some reason I hit on the idea of taking the soldiers on a visit to the local 'Spandau' brewery. I had felt it would be interesting for them to learn how beer was brewed. Accordingly, one morning I took a coach-load of about 50 troops to the brewery and for at least an hour we were given a tour and shown the full brewing process. Clearly after an hour, the troops were getting a bit restless as troops do and when the tour finally finished, they were glad to get back on the bus. We sat waiting for the driver but he didn't turn up. Instead, there was a sudden hive of activity round the main entrance and the Managing Director and his assistants appeared making their way towards us. The MD boarded the bus and started to address us all. I think we were slightly puzzled but sat patiently. He asked if we had enjoyed the visit and on being assured that we did, wondered if the troops would enjoy a quick drink. Not surprisingly there was a roar of approval.

We followed him back inside where we found tables laid for all 50 of us, with a gang of pretty Bavarian-styled waitresses, one at each table, waiting for us with jugs of beer. As soon as we sat down, the beer began to flow followed by a huge meal. I was sitting next to the MD and I remember rising to my feet and saying that I wished to thank him and his staff early in the meal for if I waited to the end as is customary, I would be quite incapable of standing up! The MD was delighted.

Fifty very happy Tankies later returned to Smuts Barracks. However, one point of this story is to note that it was now some 11 years since the war ended and there were obvious commercial reasons for the hospitality, but frankly the goodwill shown far exceeded any commercial justification for the extent and warmth of the hospitality. We had just become very good friends and no one mentioned the war!!!

Here I must mention being hosted by the 4th Hussars and their charismatic and highly respected Commanding Officer, Colonel 'Loopy' Kennard about whom a book has been written justifying his nickname. While I was there,

Bob Foreman, Recce Troop's LAD fitter. He not only fixed our vehicles and kept us on the road but featured prominently in the RTR's sporting teams.

The author toasting the German hosts at the Spandau Brewery in Berlin. I had to rush through the toast before the hospitality took effect and affected my speech.

this kindhearted commanding officer had to drive straight from an exercise to the Airport to attend a meeting at the War Office in London. He had his suitcase of civilian clothes with him on exercise.

Immediately after the exercise he was driven to Hannover Airport where he shot into a loo to change, passing his dirty uniform back over the top of the door to his driver. 'Driver, you're exhausted. Don't hang about.' 'But Sir, ...?' 'No, I'm fine, off you go.' Five minutes later Colonel Loopy emerged from the loo, immaculately suited, bowler hatted, with a rolled umbrella over his arm but without his shoes and socks. Unperturbed, this lovely man walked barefoot across the tarmac, flew to London and took a taxi to his club where the doorman, an ex-sergeant major, without batting an eyelid, phoned Col Loopy's shoemaker and arranged for a replacement pair to be sent round at the double.

Another tale of this much loved Commanding Officer occurred while I was still stationed with his regiment. The British Minister of Defence was visiting the Rhine Army and as part of his tour of the lines, he was scheduled to inspect some tanks of the 4th Hussars.

The Officers' mess at Smuts Barracks, Berlin.

About an hour or so before the visit, the Colonel was in the mess having a quiet drink when the puffy-faced divisional commander burst in demanding to see him. 'The Minister of Defence will be here at 1230. Why aren't you down at the Tank Park ensuring all is in order for the visit?'

'But General, I asked "Johnny Smith" to do this and it wouldn't be fair to be seen to be checking up on him'. Grudgingly the General left, muttering rather loudly that things had better be okay and he was now going back to divisional headquarters to meet the politician.

No one believed him and sure enough as his car left the mess, we all saw it turning, not towards Divisional HQ but to the Tank Park. Colonel Loopy thought he ought to go and check on this. Off he went and arriving at the Tank Park, he saw a very red-faced, rather paunchy General physically trying to push a tank into another position. Seeing the Colonel, he swung on him shouting 'Who is the senior officer here?' Looking quickly about and without missing a beat, Colonel Loopy replied 'I think you are, Sir'.

Back in Berlin our next-door neighbours were the Black Watch, my friends from Korea days. It was wonderful dining out with them and Eightsome Reeling after dinner. After one such dinner night, I had the worst

*Above and below*: Our days were spent on the ranges or in the training areas on navigation exercises.

*Above and right*: Star Class Racing on the Havel in Berlin.

hangover of my life. It went on for days and by the third day, I was convinced it was not just a hangover but some dreaded disease. In desperation I went to see a doctor but such was the reputation of the Black Watch he asked me straight away if I had been partying with them. When I answered in the affirmative, he said 'I thought so. Take four aspirins and you'll be OK for parade in the morning.'

Entertainment of another sort was provided on the Havel Lake and River. The army owned several marvellous yachts (more war reparations) and it gave me great pleasure taking my soldiers down in off-duty hours to teach them to sail. We had marvellous fun in the process and I was rewarded some

On exercise near Detmold with the Recce Troop.

Recce troop on the ranges at Sennelager.

40 years later when I attended the Regiment's 80th anniversary celebrations of the Battle of Cambrai. A middle-aged civilian came up to me and said 'Mr Selway, you won't remember me but you taught me to sail in Berlin in 1957 and ever since then, I have owned a boat. It's been my passion. Thank you.' The rewards for soldiering come in many ways.

We were also lucky enough to have a stable of former German Army horses, so I was able to participate in the British, American and French Horse Shows. A much more competent fellow competitor was a remarkable German 'Count' who had lost his left arm in the war. He rode an equally remarkable 'tubed' horse which made a terrifying wheezing noise as it approached each jump. The Count was very dashing and much admired by the crowd, all of whom (except his wife) seemed to know that he had a mistress. If you asked him to a party which we all did (he had that sort of charisma), you always asked which lady he would be bringing. It was on the day of the French Horse Show that he and his horse fell at the very highest, Grade A jump. Both were lying motionless on the ground when from opposite sides of the ring ran two women. They met over his prostrate body just as he was coming round. He opened one eye and quickly assessing the situation, very sensibly closed it again. The whole crowd stood in silence as he was helped off by one woman whilst his horse was led off by the other. He had become something of a star and was equally popular with the British as with the Berliners, testifying to my belief that old war time hostile attitudes can be healed if an effort is made, perhaps a lesson that can be learned today by former warring parties around the world!!

Another wonderful memory of my time in Berlin is of the East Berlin opera. Once or twice a month we went through 'Checkpoint Charlie' to see astonishing productions of world-famous operas, mainly financed by the Soviets, for which we probably paid the price of a McDonald's meal. I recall attending a performance of *Il Trovatore* where the lead was sung by the 60 year old, pre-war idol, Helge Rosvaenge. I am glad my enthusiasm is carried on by my eldest son who is something of an expert on the second half of most operas. Like other students he couldn't afford London prices for a seat so would go to a bar next door for the first half of the performance. There he would wait for the audience to come out for a drink in the interval and then mingle with them when they returned to their seats until he spied an empty one. (I thought this was a unique story until I met the charming

German lady Director of the Oman Royal Opera House who told me she had done exactly the same when she was a student.)

One visitor to our barracks in Berlin was a young Cavalry officer who in fact went on to become GOC Berlin many years later. (With his ability to seize opportunities, the reader may not be surprised at his military success.) He had been sent up on a liaison visit for a full week and immediately charmed us all. We were looking forward to working with him but after two days, he disappeared and no more was heard of him until he turned up in the mess 3 or 4 days later full of apologies. His absence was simply due to the fact that while window shopping in the famous Kurfürstendamm Avenue in Berlin, he had dawdled at a shop window selling women's lingerie and became aware of the reflection of a stunning, looking German girl. 'You think I am pretty?' she asked, which was more than enough to justify his absence.

Apart from riding and sailing, the squadron had a football team made up of great blokes but by the time I was asked to take over, they hadn't managed to win a single match. 'Well sir' said the Centre Forward, Trooper Joe Storrie, a gem of a Cockney, 'it isn't easy to play your best when you've

An American M3 Halftrack – notice the winch. These were used by the regiment for logistical support in the field, casualty evacuation and light recovery.

been on guard duty all night'. Another said, 'I'm always on cookhouse duty peeling potatoes when training is on.' The use of some PRI funds to buy smart 'Regimental' black shirts and shorts together with the cooperation of the sergeant major to control guard duty rosters, led the team to a draw in the next match and victory in every single match thereafter.

Two happy sequels to this were that I was able to bring several members of the team with me to the 3rd Tanks and many years later, as a businessman, when tasked with chasing up an urgently needed shipment from the London docks, I got into the dockyards and who should I meet but Joe Storrie, the aforementioned Centre Forward. Joe retrieved the goods in minutes – not the hours expected, with the urgent request not to mention his name to the Union if I was asked!

Sadly, the time came when it was decided to disband the Independent Squadron. We were given permission by the German authorities to mount a farewell parade and I had the good luck to lead the squadron of Comets in my jeep down the famed Olympische Strasse. I think it was the Mayor of Berlin and GOC Berlin who took the salute and the tanks turned their turrets towards them and dipped their guns as they drove past the saluting base.

It was a well-received parade and the troops did the Regiment proud. Needless to say, we were all sad to be leaving.

## Back to Detmold 'Eine wunderschöne Stadt'

I had kept in touch with Dick Ward, now a Lieutenant Colonel again and on our disbandment in Berlin, he kindly invited me to join him in the 3rd Royal Tank Regiment which he now commanded. To my delight, he offered me the plum 'glamour' job of 'OC the Recce Troop'. As mentioned earlier the Recce Troop consisted of 12 two-seater, Dingo Scout Cars. In battle they were basically located between the enemy and the leading British tanks. They were the Regiment's eyes and had to report back suggesting where the enemy might best be engaged. Thus, the crews had to be of the highest standards and in this case, several had been or were on the waiting list as potential officers.

It was midwinter when I joined and one of the first training events that I organised was an arduous fitness test walking through deep snow right

The barracks in Detmold with the RHQ on the left and the education centre and Recce Troop lines on the right.

round the celebrated Möhne Dam (of Dambuster's fame) surrounded by very steep hills.

What was memorable about this event, apart from the incredible fitness of Corporal David Buxton (later commissioned), was that on the second night, we arrived in a village and I went to see the landlord of the local Gasthof to ask if the lads could sleep in his barn. When he enquired 'are you British?', suspecting trouble, I rather warily replied 'yes'. To my

The barracks in Detmold from the Drill Square.

astonishment, he leapt to his feet, grabbed me by the hand, shook it nearly out of its socket and said in broken English that we were very welcome. He had been an anti-aircraft gunner on the dam during the raid and had never seen such bravery as the allied flight crews demonstrated that night.

He then lent us his barn and prepared an amazing dinner of steak and gallons of beer with the local villagers joining in making us all welcome. He would not let us pay a single Mark. The lads sang British songs and the villagers taught them German beer-mug-thumping songs in return. As well as a wonderful example of how war wounds can be overcome, it was a good start to team spirit building.

The Germans were generally extremely hospitable, but many were intrigued about how the British military had somehow emerged victorious over them. At a Remembrance Day parade in Paderborn, I was invited to sit on the saluting base for this annual event. After the March Past by some 10, maybe 15 different British units, I found myself standing next to the German Mayor who expressed concern that the Light Infantry always arrived late on parade. Nearly all British units marched at 120 paces to the minute and the sole exception to this is the Light Infantry who march

Möhne Dam, Corporal (later Major) David Buxton training around the Möhne Dam with Kiwi (my Labrador).

at 160 paces to the minute. They were very proud of this difference but had to go to great lengths to time their arrival at the appropriate saluting base just as the slower units finished their March Pasts. For this to work in a timely synchronised way, the parade managers had to set them off several carefully counted minutes after the main body. Spectators in the know always noted this 'difference' and would comment on the Regiment's slick timing skills. However, the mayoral sense of punctuality was mortally offended. The mayor said that he had attended this parade for several years and he simply could not understand why the Light Infantry's Colonel was never in trouble for being late and why his men always had to run to catch up. This would not have been tolerated in the German Army. When I explained, he was delighted to know that the army that beat the Wehrmacht was not as haphazard as it sometimes looked.

On one map reading exercise that ventured across Germany, we were involved in a car crash between an armoured car and a German civilian (ibid: the prelude), but even when we damaged German property, the German people accepted our presence. Generally, they were generously compensated for any damage done and farmers grew wealthy asking us to drive through their old barns and outhouses which NATO would then

On exercise near Sennelager.

rebuild. In the aftermath of the car crash in Heidelberg, we were less troubled by the car's owner than the American regional commander.

Sometimes, our miscalculations amused the Germans and mercifully, we made mistakes in an era when people were more forgiving. During an exercise in Northern Germany, I sent a scout car ahead to find a spot to pitch our tents for the night. They appeared to have found the perfect site on a wide open space covered in lush grass. They radioed us in and we immediately erected our tents and settled down for the night. In the morning I woke up, looked out of my tent and to my horror, saw that we were in the middle of a village green, surrounded by gawping locals. They were roaring with laughter as one of our troop crawled out backwards from his tent as naked as the day he was born! He stood up, stretched and opening his eyes, discovered he had an audience. I still remember the record speed with which he shot back into his tent.

The exercise was planned to take a full week and we pressed on making more overnight stops on the spectacular hill sides of the Rhine. Then 'fighting' our way south, we reached the famed Nürburgring Grand Prix Circuit located about an hour south of the city of Cologne in the heart of the Eifel mountains. All 24 Scout Cars had their moment of fame 'racing'

Dingo recce car with members of Recce Troop at Detmold.

round the circuit with its sharply banked corners. Sadly, I got cold feet when I saw the fierce competition between the Tanks and the Skins and hastily converted the 'free driving' briefing into a more conventional 'motorcade' before anybody got hurt! (But at least the crews could claim to have driven in the tracks of Stirling Moss.)

We also stopped off to pay our respects to a US regiment, the 1st Medium Tank Battalion of the 32nd Armoured Regiment based south of Frankfurt. The Colonel invited all 50 of us to supper and to kip down in the barracks afterwards. What I didn't know until the next morning was that a certain Sgt Elvis Presley was a member of that regiment and that night the Brits received a full hour's sing along with him in their barrack rooms. Lucky lads.

Under Dick Ward, the Regiment took its sports very seriously. He understood its role in engendering teamwork and effectiveness and in a peacetime army he saw sport as a way to maintain the regiment's sharpness and profile. I was given time to compete in the 1958 divisional Ski Championships held in Austria and since I did quite well, though I say it myself, I was authorised to create a team to compete in the 1959 and 1960 Army Championships.

A few hours later we were 'bogged' in. If there was soft mud anywhere we were magnetically drawn to it. German mud; no wonder they built autobahns!

Dogs were practically part of the uniform in those days and nearly every officer had one. There was an established pecking order in the Mess as far as canine seating was concerned. Those belonging to the senior subalterns were allowed to occupy the most comfortable chairs and woe betide any miserable junior subaltern who tried to turf them out. They were left to stand or sit on the most uncomfortable furniture in the room well away from the fire.

As a senior subaltern at that stage, my black Labrador bitch Kiwi sometimes let my seniority in the Officers' Mess go to her head. I had developed a passion for show jumping and was proud to win several rosettes. My summer days centred round getting up at 5.30 to train with the lovely 'Snaffles' (an army horse) for an hour or so. Kiwi and I would be greeted by a whinny and off we would go, Kiwi often showing the way, making sure she took a wet route wherever possible. After the ride, she would stay in my room while I showered. On returning to my room, I would invariably find a large wet patch right in the middle of my bed and a black dog lying on the floor feigning sleep. When challenged, she was always most hurt that I could even suggest she would be so disobedient as to get up

Dingo racing at the world famous Nürburgring racetrack!

A Dingo out on forward recce for the Regiment. Our role was to provide an observation screen and to sound out routes and obstacles for the heavier tanks. Wheels gave us speed and created less noise but limited our movement to firmer ground.

on my bed. 70 years later I can still see her look of innocence when she was shown the wet patch! How I loved that dog!!

Meanwhile Snaffles and I got very fit with these early sessions and the peak of our success came when I was announced as the winner of the 1959 Army Hunter Trials. In this I recall thundering down a slope towards the biggest jump I had ever attempted, closing my eyes and saying 'Go it girl, it's all yours' and we sailed over the hurdle as if it were a small practice jump. What a lady!! However, what I most remember was the generous praise I received from my peers – mainly belonging to cavalry regiments, who bought bottle after bottle of champagne. This was true comradeship and sportsmanship for to an extent this was traditionally their territory and I had trodden on it!!

Then disappointingly about 45 minutes later, in the middle of these celebrations, the stewards announced that there had been a radio breakdown at one of the fences at which I had incurred four faults and therefore slipped to second. But what to me couldn't be taken away was the comradeship shown by my competitors and along the way I had enhanced the reputation of my Regiment and the approval of my boss.

Sharing my enthusiasm for riding was a newly joined 2nd Lt W. A. (Tony) Allen. He rapidly became the most popular subaltern in the Regiment due to the number of 'extra orderly officer duties' he received! Later he took over from me as equitation officer, scoring yet another extra orderly officer duty when he arrived at the stables on his first morning 30 minutes after the Colonel! After this shaky start, he went on to command a regiment and later in retirement, he and his wife built a successful market garden business which he eventually sold for a vast sum. Not wishing to be idle, he then became boss of the Red Cross in Norfolk and also wrote articles for the magazine *Country Life* amongst other publications.

Culturally we weren't starved and on one occasion I persuaded several of my troop (as unlikely opera buffs as one can imagine) to attend a local Bielefeld opera performance of the *Bartered Bride*. This had one unexpected result. Some 55 years later, I attended the funeral of one of my ex-soldiers in the north of England. There was another of my former soldiers present, Lance Corporal Jack Jenkins, who remembered that night very well. He told me he had never been to an opera before and despite not understanding a word, loved every minute of it. Indeed, he so enjoyed his introduction to opera that

On exercise somewhere in Germany. A well-camouflaged Dingo waits patiently to be driven into some deep mud.

Snaffles going though her paces at the Divisional Championships.

he became an avid supporter and later a director of Scottish Opera! I was very touched when he added that he would have hated his National Service had it not been for the activities we got up to in our Recce Troop.

Needless to say, I loved my time with the troop. It was very rewarding to see that while trying to get them 'war ready', I had also succeeded in making soldiering fun. It was nice to know you got it right sometimes!

Meanwhile training continued seriously and I was very proud of the lads when they won the title of 'Champion Troop'. Their overall enthusiasm was contagious. They formed the core of several inter-regimental team sporting events such as sailing at the British Kiel Yacht club in the Baltic and skiing in both the divisional and the Army Ski Championships held in Austria which included both downhill and military cross country (Langlauf).

Here in 1960, we won the divisional Ski Championships. We might well have gone on to win the Army Championships if Capt Hugh Wingfield Hayes hadn't sadly broken his leg on the final rundown to the start of the downhill races. His place was taken by a gallant member of the cross country team. Such is luck but our heads were held high when we came in 2nd! This excellence in professional and extracurricular achievement bears out Dick Ward's belief that sport enhances soldiering.

At this stage I must sing the praises of David Mallam. He had won the Sword of Honour at Sandhurst and was clearly a natural leader. We saw eye to eye on most things and when he said he would like to get involved in our skiing activities, I was delighted. He had never skied before but he was a natural sportsman and very keen to try. At this time the cross-country team was captained by Lt Robert Gieve of the well known Savile Row military tailors. No one could have shown more guts than he but by the end

RTR team – cross country at Winterberg – divisional competition in 1958/9.

1959. Ehrwald, Austria, under the Zugspitze. Regiment members training for the ski team. The selection process for the ski team was very competitive. From this initial cadre, daily eliminations reduced the team to its core 4 members. We pioneered the 'Strictly' elimination model decades before it was a TV trope.

of the first 20 km heat, his team had to help the still determined but totally exhausted Robert over the finishing line.

Sadly, for such a great guy, he just couldn't go on. David, as strong as an ox, came to the rescue volunteering to take over if I agreed. He had never cross country skied in his life but believed 'Langlaufing is just like walking but easier' and proved it by bringing the team in first in the next heat and going on to win the divisional championships! It was pure determination and certainly not practise that got him to the front.

Most officers in the early 50s had an unsigned social contract or understanding, that in return for poor salaries (compared to our civilian counterparts) and facing the risks of combat, we led a heavily subsidised and privileged life with sport, comradeship and a certain 'leeway' with resources.

Until the establishment of the Army Air Corps in 1957, the tank regiments had dedicated air support that was a part of its reconnaissance screen. These aircraft also taxied the brass around and were used for supporting the squadrons. In the run up to a major competition at Winterberg, I had asked

*Right and below*: Winterberg – with the Final RTR Ski Team. We won the Army Ski Championship much to the annoyance of the Cavalry who hated being beaten by us!

the regimental tailors at the last minute to make us new team ski suits but they were not ready by the time we left for the competition. A simple and visible mistake that would have reflected poorly on my organisational skills if I had not been fortunate enough to have a friend, Stephen Love, who was a spotter for the Royal Artillery's air observation post. He would later be the defence attache in Buenos Aires and hosted General Mario Menéndez at a dinner party on the night before the South Georgia and Falklands Invasion. At midnight the General had stood up from the table, apologised for what was about to happen and left.

At that time Stephen's role was to pilot small single-seater Auster aircraft for forward air observation. Because I didn't want to draw internal attention to my inefficiency, he kindly flew an unsanctioned mission to Winterberg to

Princess Marina, the Duchess of Kent, presented prizes at Winterberg for the Army Ski Championships.

deliver our ski suits. He did this by flying over us numerous times in 'bombing runs' and throwing out the tightly bound packages of ski suits, trying to hit us. Luckily for the team, like most Gunners, he missed. These 'perks' of service were already starting to dry up by the middle of the 50s and the reduction in the size of the Army and particularly the tank regiments, which were amalgamating to reduce the number of regiments to five, then four (and now one) was starting to bite. Budgetary concerns were also cutting into the opportunities to exercise at will across Germany and much of the Officer's roles were refocused on saving money rather than saving Europe. The Army was downsizing, perhaps understandably given the economic pressures, but the role of command was also reflecting these squeezes. Commanders like Dick Ward who appreciated the military value of sport fought a rear guard action to indulge team building opportunities wherever possible despite the economic constraints. Their legacy endures every Wednesday afternoon in most regiments.

A lifelong friendship began around this time with fellow officer, Hugo Brooke. Together we enjoyed healthy 'extracurricular' activities and regimental balls for which dancing partners were invited over from

*Above left, above right and right*: The Army Air Corps used a variety of aircraft to support the army. The value of helicopters was still being examined.

England. We amassed many miles in my new Sunbeam Rapier, including a trip to Sweden.

Later that year with Hugo co-driving and map reading and me driving, we won a regimental motor rally against competitors from the Skins and the 9th Lancers. That rallying sparked an interest in Hugo that led to him winning the Army Driving Championship twice over the next four years, the first with the Army Air Corps as the individual winner and the second with the 3rd Royal Tank Regiment as the team winners.

*Above left and above right*: British Kiel Yacht Club, an Army sailing club that was stocked almost exclusively with requisitioned yachts from the German Army.

Hugo Brooke went on to win the Army Driving Championships. I was especially honoured to be the best man at each of his four weddings.

*Left and below*: Training at Winterberg.

## The Arctic

After the Army ski champinships, my team were invited to join in an ad hoc 'Ski Company' scheduled to provide 'enemy' to the Norwegian Army up in the Arctic Circle. There were 55 men in the detachment which was the largest group of British soldiers ever to train with the Norwegian Army under these conditions. Guarding NATO's Northern border required special training and in the early Cold War era, the Army's skiers and Commandos were the obvious candidates. It also seemed a great opportunity to challenge a recce troop and shortly afterwards we flew north to Tromsø in a 'Blackburn Beverley' aircraft which seemed huge at the time.

MANOEUVRES IN THE ARCTIC. Members of 1 (British) Corps Independent Ski Detachment formed from British units in Germany, outside their tents, which they set up in the mountains three miles north of the Arctic Circle while taking part recently in the Norwegian Army's winter manoeuvre Roede Orme. There were 55 men in the detachment which was the largest group of British soldiers ever to train with the Norwegian Army under such conditions.

Gales and heavy snow were experienced during the exercise, and patrols encountered conditions in which driving snow reduced visibility to nil. When the men returned to their base camp at [illegible], in Northern Norway, they were in high spirits. The only casualty in the detachment was one man suffering from toothache.

Manoeuvres in the Arctic. Members of 1(British) Corps Independent Ski Detachment formed from British units in Germany, outside their tents which they set up in the mountains, three miles North of the Arctic Circle, while taking part in the Norwegian Army's winter manoeuvre 'Roede Orme'. Gales and heavy snow were experienced during the exercise and patrols encountered conditions in which driving snow reduced visibility to nil.

We were met by the Norwegian Army and the subsequent warm relationship was perhaps set by their handouts of 'useful phrases' which included extremely relevant comments such as 'the enemy are attacking from the right', interspersed with equally useful phrases such as 'Your sister is very pretty. Can I meet her?'!!

On one occasion during an exercise, acting as the enemy forces, we assaulted a group of Norwegian soldiers in a defensive position in a valley below us. As we came skiing down on them in a straight line, they rather disappointingly took not a blind bit of notice. Then just as we reached them, they bent down, grabbed the tips of our skis and skilfully flipped us over so that we landed on our backs in a helpless undignified heap. Then sitting on our chests they gently urged us to 'go home filthy British'!

The British team were all accomplished skiers but for some extraordinary reason, somebody had thought to appoint an infantry major who could barely ski to command the company. He became a seriously inept, indeed

The author with Recce Troop members on exercise 'Roede Orme' – we wore berets instead of warm practical ski wear.

*Above left and above right*: We experimented with moving troops across country and spent some time seeing if towing troops was feasible. Being towed by a halftrack seemed a good idea in theory but in practise didn't work well initially. After a few tries we began to master the technique, but if one fell... it could get messy.

dangerous, boss, more than likely to put lives at risk on the avalanche-prone hill sides. At this stage it became clear that as the second senior officer, I somehow had to control him. My fellow officers put much pressure on me to get him removed and after one very dangerous order, actually advised me to arrest him. Though unpleasant I felt we could handle the situation and so it remained, but it left a nasty taste.

Overall however, it was a hugely successful episode with lots of goodwill and many serious lessons learned in winter warfare. When it came time to leave and we were queuing to board the Beverley, a large number of our Norwegian friends came to see us off. Suddenly from behind their backs they unleashed a torrent of snowballs accompanied by shouts of 'Go home filthy British!' to which we rapidly responded with equally plentiful snowballs and insults of a ribald nature.

On return to Germany, I learned that the 3rd and 6th Tanks were destined to merge and that a major parade was to be held to mark the event. The amalgamation took place at Sennelager on 13 October 1959 and the parade was taken by a former Commanding Officer of the Third, Lt Gen Sir Harold Pyman, KCB, CBE, DSO, who was then the Colonel Commandant, RTR.

The 3rd and 6th had much common history, having been brigaded together in 1917, when they were still known as 'C' and 'F' Battalions, of the Tank Corps. Later in 1917, they were the first units to receive the new

Whippet tank. In the Second World War they had fought side by side at Sidi Rezegh and Alamein and more recently, at Suez. We used the airstrip at Sennelager as our parade ground and the old windmill which stands beside the strip was painted in Regimental colours. A mounted, armoured parade took place, sadly in mist and rain.

A film was made at the time and I do recommend that if anyone is interested in seeing what operational life was like in 1959, they look for it on YouTube.

The film not only shows the 'Merger Parade' but includes tanks training, the daily routine and a couple of shots of Colonel Dick Ward. Watching it in 2023, it brings back vivid memories of Detmold and the five wonderful years I spent there.

# Chapter 8

# Conclusions

*'You have taught me that there are three ways of doing things in this world the Right way, the Wrong way, and the Selway'*
*A quote by a very patient Army boss.*

Sadly, at this time, my widowed father had a stroke and lost his ability to speak, but not his thought process or his zest for life. He was transferred from nursing home to nursing home but it was clear that my presence was needed back in the UK. The doctors judged him fit in all other aspects and the prognosis was that he would live for several years to come, so it was agreed both in the family and the regiment that I should apply for one of the 'golden bowlers' being offered and leave the Army at the end of March 1960.

After serving since 1947, what was I to do with my life? Here I received a marvellous stroke of luck. Through riding and other activities, I had got to know Col Christie Becket, the colonel of the 9th Lancers, the adjacent Regiment. He very kindly fixed for me to meet a good friend of his, John King, later Lord King of British Airways fame. Lord King offered me a management trainee job in his ball bearing factory in Northampton at a salary well ahead of expectations. I gladly accepted and in June 1960, I took up my first civilian post.

In my later years, I have often wondered how my military career might have developed had I not had to resign due to the illness of my widowed father. Perhaps with Dick Ward's support, I might have achieved a level of success that would have made my parents proud! I would have loved to have commanded a regiment and ensured they were champions in all that they did! However, aged 31, I was committed to start a new life as a civilian!

For my last five years with the Regiment, I had secured gradings of 'Above Average' in four of my five annual reports linked to recommendations for promotion to Major and entry to the Staff College. I had faced 'active service' in Korea and not been found wanting. Indeed, I had been promoted ahead of two senior colleagues in a very competitive environment with few promotion opportunities before a forecast major battle and had been called to my Squadron HQ to understudy my (now revered) boss Major Richard Ward, whose confidence I had secured. (A confidence that lasted during his life when he invited me to become Godfather to one of his children.)

I had won sporting trophies at Divisional level in Sailing, Skiing, Show Jumping and Cross Country Eventing as well as gaining the coveted 'Champion Troop' trophy for the 3rd Tanks.

After leaving the Tank Regiment, I served with the Inns of Court, a Yeomanry unit within the Territorial Army which was equipped with armoured cars, but after a few years the demands of my business took me to the Middle East where I worked in the UAE, Qatar and Bahrain before settling in the Sultanate of Oman. Frustratingly, Covid complicated work and my residence in Oman and in 2020, at the age of 93, I retired and moved back to England where I now live with my long-suffering wife, Deirdre, near two of my four sons and my eight grandchildren.

At this stage and upon reflection, I would like to share the following conclusions about the Korean war and offer a general view about the value of this war in particular, the lessons it has for our young generations and a few words about the personal rewards of my service that have lasted a lifetime.

## The Value of Experience and Leadership

I have gone on at length about the Regiment's senior officers, especially those with Second World War service and how their experience shaped the daily service of enlisted and junior officers in Korea. These veterans had considerable practical experience of combat situations and were able to share more than their tactical knowledge with younger soldiers. They served as mentors and role models for younger soldiers and offered guidance on both professional and personal matters. For example, their wartime experience also taught them to use humour, sometimes dark, to make light of difficult tasks but also as a coping mechanism to offset the horror of the conflict. The horrors of First World War shell shock, as it was known, which has become post traumatic stress, were less familiar around Korean veterans despite the brutality of the Korean War. The bloodshed that I and our troops observed after the Chinese human wave attacks and the brutal impact of our artillery was no less horrific than anything seen in either WW1 or WW2, but somehow traumatised us less than those or more recent conflicts seem to. Certainly there was less awareness of this among Korean veterans I have met and spoken with. I think we can largely attribute this to the mentorship of these highly-seasoned campaigners who led us through relatively unscathed. In short, they were able to share their 'coping mechanisms' with their troops.

A strong factor in the mental welfare of our troops was the understanding that the war was justified, by both the UN, who we represented, and by general public opinion and especially among the people of South Korea. That we understood the virtue of our cause was a direct result of our senior officers instilling within us the broader political and societal issues that we were fighting for. PTSD, as we understand and refer to it now, was far from unknown in survivors of the Korean War, but occurred less within units with strong morale and these units were typically enriched with strong seasoned leadership. The causes and virtues of the Vietnam War, by contrast, were not as well understood by the US combatants, in a war when so many other factors were equal and I believe this is why the incidence of PTSD was higher. As the Cold War progressed and devolved into the War on Terror, conflicts saw fewer WW2 or experienced veterans in regimental positions which I believe is a factor in the increased mental toll that wars take. I certainly don't remember anyone suffering from PTSD in Korea.

The Amalgamation Parade between the 3rd and 6th Royal Tank Regiments.

Their presence also helped younger soldiers navigate the psychological and emotional demands of the job, which promoted mental resilience. Veterans had experience adapting to different environments and situations, which was critical in the rapidly changing and unpredictable combat scenarios in Korea.

I have also gone on at length about the use of sport, in wartime, as much as peace and the apparent obsession for instilling a sense of normality and routine, such as conducting sports afternoons, church parades, exotic leave, relaxing weekends and ceremonial parades, almost within Chinese artillery range. This apparent indifference to the war was exemplified by the continuation of parades, coronation events and even maintaining normal work week/weekend routines. This apparent absurdity was not only beneficial for its role in promoting health, fitness and teamwork, but senior command also understood its value as a method of distracting and de-escalating the mental impact of stress from the war.

## The Value of the Forgotten War

During the Korean War the Regiment was permanently in action for five months of the nine we were there. In this time, it had fired 23,800 rounds from its main armament, received 68 direct hits on its tanks and suffered 20 casualties, one of whom was killed. It is vexing that this conflict, albeit geographically remote and overshadowed by the Second World War and Vietnam, is overlooked by many. I think this might reflect the success of the United Nations effort rather than the conflict's lack of relevance.

Although most of us first learned of our posting to Korea with mixed feelings, there are few of us who do not look back on it now as a great and valuable experience. We became proficient in an unusual and specialised form of warfare; we met and made friends with many people, not only from all over the Commonwealth but also from many corners of the world; we lived in a strange and little known country; we fought in a unique and remarkable Army which carried the flags of seventeen nations; and above all we took an active and honourable part in stemming the advance of Communism. It was a year packed with interest and we took away with us memories which will live for years to come.

Sadly, I am the last surviving Royal Tank Regiment officer who fought in the Korean War but I remain in contact with some members of my troop who have contributed to these pages and share certain conclusions about our joint experiences. Firstly, a frustration that the Korean War is not recognised for either its importance to world peace, its scale, or its brutality. According to Max Hastings, the war remains one of the most significant, compelling clashes of arms in this century. The war was bitterly disputed and of the 1,319,000 Americans that served in the Korean theatre, 33,629 did not return. A further 105,785 were wounded. The South Korean army lost 415,000 killed and 429,000 wounded. The Commonwealth – Britain, Canada, Australia and New Zealand – lost 1,263 killed and 4,817 wounded. Belgium, Colombia, Ethiopia, France, Greece, Holland, the Philippines, Thailand and Turkey between them lost 1,800 killed and 7,000 wounded, of whom almost half were Turks. It is estimated that more than 1.5 million Chinese and North Koreans died in the conflict.

Nobody looking at North and South Korea today can doubt that the West's intervention in 1950 saved the Southerners from a tragic fate and indeed opened the way to a future that was infinitely better than is available in the North. The war also revitalised NATO, allowed it to develop close military cooperation with its members, something I believe the Soviet armies never managed, and hastened the divide between China and the Soviet Union and members of the Warsaw Pact. I believe that each of these was reason enough to justify our support of South Korea, a republic that still values our contribution, even if our own government has reprioritised its focus.

A Korean peasant's funeral. Life was hard enough, without a war.

This was a war that deserves our attention, if for no other reasons than there are lessons that we are in danger of forgetting and threats that we overlook today. It was the last large-scale, casualty-intensive war we have fought. This is not to understate the contributions and sacrifices of British soldiers since or the intensity of the conflicts since but they have been limited or asymmetric. We see in Ukraine now a scale of European war that breaks a 70-year tradition of comparative peace and I worry that we have forgotten the lessons from this forgotten war, especially the importance of human leadership in these automated times. I hope this story stresses the value of experience.

1 RTR arrived in Korea while the truce negotiations were underway, but the fighting continued for months after a military stalemate was acknowledged by both sides. Mainly motivated for supposed propaganda gains, the Chinese launched several attacks which promised no strategic gains yet caused thousands of needless deaths. Astonishingly 1 RTR lost one man killed and several wounded, however I lost several friends from the infantry companies that bore the brunt of the casualties. Our low casualty rates reflected our leaders' restraint and adversity to needless risk-taking. 45 per cent of all US casualties happened after the first armistice negotiations opened with the Communists. Luckily, our leadership, schooled in the Second World War, rejected personal glory and made a virtue of restraint. Our young blood was keen for excitement and success, and as a technically superior force, even if outnumbered, it was difficult to not get frustrated, and to acknowledge the rationality of maintaining a static war. The UN and South Korea were winning the peace and there was little need for extra heroics. Ultimately, the nuclear threat was a risk the Chinese dared not match but it was as much the threat of a conventional assault from our superior force that forced the truce terms through, and the UN victory lies in holding out for terms which embarrassed the Chinese narrative for the war. The moral for future leaders is clear. Have the moral courage to do what you believe to be right and stand by your decisions. Even if this means sometimes not fighting.

## The Comradeship

I hope these memories of my time in the static conditions in the frontline give an indication of what it was like in the spring and early summer of 1953, and my accounts of serving with the Royal Tank Regiment throughout the 1950s gives a feel for the life of a subaltern then. Predominantly it was a time of generating exceptional long-term friendships with fellow Tankies and infantry with whom we shared apprehensive yet exhilarating experiences. I was proud that I earned the respect and thanks of Robert MacGregor Oldfield (later Brigadier) who, as a Subaltern in the DLI leading one such patrol, called for and received swift support from a RTR Centurion that extracted his patrol out of very serious trouble.

I had always felt that I had had a good and exciting 'war' in Korea and 'done my bit' but researching for this memoir and a proposed anthology of heroism during this war has both delighted and humbled me for I have come across stories written by comrades, many of whom I knew, that highlight exceptional feats of bravery and comradeship that went unmentioned at the time. These accounts really show what soldiering and the war in Korea, was about.

Of the finest friends I made over my army career, my own tank crews in Korea and fellow officers are firmly lodged into those most cherished ranks. These guys are not forgotten and are amongst the many to whom I am indebted for inspiring me then and in later life. Sadly, either space limitations in this memoir, a loss of contact or for their own modesty or for the sake of the families, some of the more sensational anecdotes concerning the departed are omitted; after all, '*De mortuis nil nisi bonum dicendum est*'!

My brother officers were also a source of strength and appear throughout this book. There were countless examples of comradeship trumping discipline, the example of Stephen Love flying my team's ski trousers exemplifies the strength of the bonds we formed.

These friendships were maintained throughout my life and remain a source of constant pleasure and pride for me as I followed their interests and welfare. To name a few, Hugo Brooke is a leading expert on moths and one of my corporals became a director of a national opera company. The common thread among us all is the Regiment and our time in service together; a fraction of our life spans, sometimes less than a year of shared experiences but closer bonds were not replicated throughout the rest of our civilian lives.

I was living and working in the Sultanate of Oman when I started writing this memoir. Here I was astonished and humbled when I learned of the huge and continued gratitude shown by the Korean people for what the West did between 1950 and 1953. I met the then Korean Ambassador to Oman and

The Korean Ambassador to Oman and the Military Attaché with the Author and his wife Deidre in Muscat, Oman.

Dick Ward (left), squadron officers and the author (Right). I am amazed when I compare this picture to the same group the previous December in Pusan. I never dreamt I would have my hands in my pockets in Dick Ward's company. The relief of emerging from the conflict partly accounts for the relaxed poses but the experience had changed us all.

when I mentioned my Korean War Scrapbook, he immediately invited me to the Embassy so that he could have a look at it. From then on, while we were still in Oman, we were honoured guests at all their national events including the opening of their new Embassy and a Reception for their

National Day celebrations onboard a Korean warship on R&R from anti-piracy patrols in the Arabian Gulf. On that occasion, to our embarrassment, we found ourselves being piped aboard and treated with as much respect as all the official Omani bemedalled guests.

I remember talking to one young female ship's officer at the reception. When she learned of my involvement in 1953, she said how honoured she

James (Jim) and Deirdre (Dumpy) Selway in August 2023, England on their 50th wedding anniversary.

was to meet me and that she had learned at school all about the war and the sacrifices made. Her attitude reflected the views of many Koreans that I met in later life.

The Embassy and the Ship's crew were not the only ones to honour us in this way. Every now and again, the Korean Businessmen's Association would turn up with boxes of Korean pears and bunches of flowers and during Covid, multiple packets of masks and gloves.

Back in the UK, through communication with more and more Korean veterans via a very vibrant Facebook group, the British Korean Veterans' Association, I realised this gratitude was directed at everyone who served there. Indeed in 2020, all survivors who could be traced received a Commemoration Plaque from the Korean Embassy in the UK.

It is very humbling. Surely no other nation has thanked the West for their efforts and sacrifices as much as the Koreans. Veterans visiting the country continually tell me of how warmly they were treated.

Perhaps our true reward is shown most clearly by the astonishing growth of this dynamic nation, especially when contrasted, through the prism of the 38th Parallel, with the North. Who could not look at the primitive Korea we experienced in the 1950s and the Korea of today and not be awed? This growth alone justified our undertakings. I can only hope that our struggles contributed to a more enduring peace on the Korean Peninsula.

The author (Back left) with his troop on the 38th Parallel.

# Glossary

| | |
|---|---|
| ADC | Aide de Camp |
| Bde/Bgd | Brigade |
| Britcom | British and Commonwealth Brigade |
| Bt | Battalion |
| BW | Black Watch |
| DF | Defensive Fire |
| Div | Division (i.e ROK Div) |
| DLI | Durham Light Infantry |
| Dukes | The Duke of Wellington's Regiment |
| DFL | Forward Defensive Lines |
| Inf | Infantry |
| KSR | Korean Service Regiment |
| MC | Military Cross |
| MLR | Main Line of Resistance |
| MSR | Main Supply Route |
| POW | Prisoners of War |
| ROK | Republic of Korea, the main body of the South Korean forces |
| RAR | Royal Australian Regiment, battalions, 1 RAR, 2 RAR etc. |
| RASC | Royal Army Service Corps |
| RNZAC | Royal New Zealand Armoured Corps |
| RTR | Royal Tank Regiment |
| R&R | Rest and Recreation |
| Skins | 5th Inniskilling Dragoon Guards |
| Sqn | Squadron |
| SHQ | Squadron Headquarters |
| Tp | Troop |
| UN | United Nations |
| PVA | People's Volunteer Army, the main Chinese forces. |

# Appendix A

# 1st Royal Tank Regiment Order of Battle 1952

This is the original published list of Officers who set off to Korea but sadly does not include those who joined us from the Commonwealth once we were 'in station'.

**RHQ.**

| | | | |
|---|---|---|---|
| CO | Lt Col | GC. | Hopkinson, DSO, MC |
| 2 i/c | Major | HPS. | Massy |
| Adjt | Capt | DVA. | Ambridge, MC |
| A/Adjt | Lieut | MAV. | Rickatson |
| RSO | Lieut | RMH. | Vickers |
| IO | Lieut | TJC. | Cockman |
| RHQ Tp | Lieut | TSM. | Welch |
| LO | Capt | PR. | Wilson |
| RTA | Major | WDP. | Sullivan, MBE |

**HQ SQN**

| | | | |
|---|---|---|---|
| OC | Major | JBB. | Ferguson |
| 2i/c | Capt | SB. | Ferguson |
| RTO | Capt | DG. | Horton |
| PRI | Capt | KC. | Dudley |
| QM | Capt | J. | Taylor, MBE, MM |
| Recce Tp | 2/Lieut | PS. | Berry |
| EME | Capt | WJ. | Exley |
| 2 i/c LAD | Lieut | VV. | O'Shea |
| RMO | Lieut | OP. | Galpin (RAMC) |

**A SQN**

| | | | |
|---|---|---|---|
| OC | Major | SI. | Howard Jones, DSO, MC |
| 2 i/c | Capt | JD. | Brotchie, MC |
| | Capt | AE. | Simmons, MC |
| | Lieut | MFV. | Jackson |
| | Lieut | DC. | Crouch |
| | Lieut | PD. | Fanshawe (Bays) |
| | 2/Lieut | PF. | Bede Cox |
| | 2/Lieut | JN. | Busk |

**B SQN**

| | | | |
|---|---|---|---|
| OC | Major | RE. | Ward, DSO, MC |
| 2 i/c | Major | VJ. | Senior, MC |
| | Capt | AH. | Thrift, MC |
| | Lieut | CGP. | Snowden |
| | Lieut | MH. | Sinnatt |
| | Lieut | MG. | Farmer |
| | Lieut | JA. | Selway |
| | 2/Lieut | M. | Colston (17/21 L) |

**C SQN**

| | | | |
|---|---|---|---|
| OC | Major | RE. | Maunsell, MC |
| 2 i/c | Capt | RP. | Barker |
| | Capt | JA. | Cowgill |
| | Lieut | AC. | Uloth |
| | 2/Lieut | JD. | Bastick |
| | 2/Lieut | JR. | Chapman |
| | 2/Lieut | SDE. | Lewis |

**Not initially allocated to Squadrons**

| | | | |
|---|---|---|---|
| | Capt | JPL. | Caunter |
| | Lieut | JDS. | Henderson |
| | Lieut | JB. | Benrum |
| | Lieut | ME. | Roberts |
| | Lieut | G. | Forty |
| | Lieut | R. | Beard |
| | 2/Lieut | PS. | Anthill |
| | 2/Lieut | TJ. | Thomas |
| | 2/Lieut | JL. | Damant (7th H) |

## The Korean Journal. First Royal Tank Regiment 1952-53

### September 1952

The Regiment left Germany on 2nd September 1952, after having served there continuously since the day it crossed the German frontier at the head of 21 Army Group in the closing stages of the Second World War. On arrival in England it was quartered in Fowler Barracks, Perham Down where the final kitting and organisation for Korea was carried out and from where the last period of leave was taken.

### October and November 1952

The Regiment set sail from Liverpool in H.M.T. *Empire Halladale* on 27th October. Major General N. Duncan the Representative Colonel Commandant and many other RTR officers came to the port to wish all ranks farewell and the Cambrai Band played the Regiment away, as the *Empire Halladale* steamed down the Mersey.

The voyage was memorable chiefly for an Atlantic gale which received headlines in the papers and drove the fishing fleets to ports, the lavish entertainment provided by the 'Seventh' in Hong Kong and the slowness of the *Empire Halladale.*

### December 1952

The Regiment arrived at Pusan early on the morning of 6th December. There we saw for the first time the bleak and barren Korean hills which were to be our constant companions for the next 12 months. At midday the Regiment received an official welcome from a large reception committee headed by a Cabinet Minister of the Republic of Korea, the British Minister in Korea and high ranking United States Officers of the United Nations Command. After several speeches of welcome, the CO was presented with a bouquet of flowers by a small and brightly attired Korean girl.

The Regiment disembarked the next day and travelled North in a desperately cold, hard, wooden-seated, American-run troop train which had no heating and windows which had little glass remaining. A very sorry party got off the train at Tokchon the following morning at 8 a.m., only to find that there were still further trials ahead, in the form of an hour and a half in the backs of draughty trucks, over rough and dusty roads.

Such things, however, were soon forgotten as there were only 24 hours to take over from the 5th Royal Inniskilling Dragoon Guards, who had two Squadrons in action in the line. On the early morning of the 9th December they mounted their vehicles, to start on their long journey to warmer climes and the Regiment found itself once more in action, after 7 years of peacetime soldiering.

The 1st Commonwealth Division was holding its sector of the front with its three Brigades in the line, each Brigade having a battalion in reserve.

On the left was 25 Canadian Infantry Brigade with 'B' Squadron Lord Strathcona's Horse in support, who came under operational control of the Regiment. The central sector was held by 29 British Infantry Brigade, with 'B' Squadron commanded by Major Ward in support and the right sector by 28 Britcom Infantry Brigade with 'A' Squadron commanded by Major Howard Jones in support. 'C' Squadron commanded by Major Maunsell went into Divisional reserve, South of the River Imjin.

The Squadrons in the line were deployed with just over half their tanks dug in, in the frontline, closely integrated in the infantry defensive plan. Their tasks were to harass the enemy by day, by destroying Command Posts and defence works and prevent all forms of daylight movement. By night their tasks were fire close in DFs in the front of infantry positions to deal with enemy raids and attacks and to fire prearranged tasks in support of friendly patrols. In these tasks tanks proved invaluable and formed an essential part of the Brigade defensive plans.

At this time the Korean winter was in full swing and the Regiment had to acclimatise itself very quickly to the bitter cold after its voyage through tropical seas. It was very soon discovered that for the solitary watcher on the hill tops, no colder place could be found than a tank which contrives to funnel the wind into its innermost parts and freezes its crew with the mass of cold metal with which it envelopes them.

Amongst the many problems imposed by the cold, the cooking of breakfast was one of the most tiresome. All normal liquids are solid, eggs have to be peeled off their shells instead of broken and must be thawed before they can be fried and milk has to be served with a knife.

The front at this time proved to be comparatively quiet. However, it was not long before all tanks that were in position in the line had had their first taste of Chinese shell fire and although this was never heavy, it was liable to arrive without warning at any time of the day and consequently kept the crews on their toes.

On the night of 10th December 'A' Squadron supported a raid on the enemy lines by a Company of the 1st Bn Royal Australian Regiment which made a deep penetration, returning before light the next day.

A tank of 'A' Squadron, commanded by an Australian Officer, got itself into the news and below is a copy of a cutting from the *Daily Express*:

> Two British Centurions of the Royal Tank Regiment one ablaze and filled with choking fumes silenced a big Chinese gun concealed in a deep tunnel in a hillside in Korea. The tanks were under the command of an Australian, Lieutenant D.J. Duff of Melbourne, an Australian officer gaining experience with the Tank Regiment. The tunnel gun opened up on the Centurions which were in fixed positions giving support to front line troops. The tank under Duff's command was the only one manned at the time. 'The Chinese were firing mortars and 75s,' he said. 'Their mortar fire was accurate and a direct hit on my tank started a fire in some material on top. This forced my crew to withdraw. The crew of the other Centurion crawled up to their tank and into the turret opening, one by one, dodging the shell bursts.'
>
> Then they opened fire on the entrance to the tunnel which housed the Chinese Gun. The Centurion's 20 pounder shells entered the tunnel and burst so deep in the hill that the explosions could not be seen.
>
> Lieutenant Duff said, 'Five bombs hit one of the Centurions but left it undamaged.' Reuters.

**January 1953**

During the month of January, the deployment of the Regiment remained unchanged. The front remained comparatively quiet, though the Regiment took part in three small operations. In the early hours of 12th January 'B' Squadron provided supporting fire for a raiding party from 1st Bn The Duke of Wellington's Regiment which was attempting to capture a prisoner. In this it was unsuccessful but returned without casualties.

On 24th January a Troop of 'B' Squadron and one from 'C' Squadron which had moved up into the 'B' Squadron sector, supported another raiding party from 1st Bn The Duke of Wellington's Regiment which assaulted an enemy-held feature in daylight, in order to blow in a tunnel and capture a prisoner. The tunnel was successfully blown but only one dead Chinese soldier was brought back. In both these small actions the 'Dukes' reported that the tank fire was extremely accurate and of the greatest value, both in helping them to reach their objectives and to withdraw unmolested.

On 26th January a tank of 'C' Squadron, fitted with special track wedges to enable it to climb over the frozen ground, moved up into the line in the sector held by the 3rd Bn The Royal Australian Regiment. At first light it climbed forward into an exposed position from where it was able to fire into some tunnels on the reverse slopes of enemy position. After firing 34 rounds of HE, the commander reported that the tunnels were severely damaged and withdrew for breakfast to 'A' Squadron's Headquarters.

**February and March 1953**

At the beginning of the month of February, the Commonwealth Division and with it the Regiment was withdrawn from the line, their place being taken by the 2nd U.S. Division. This was a severe blow after having been in action for so short a time and was furthermore a considerable problem. A very varied assortment of highly mobile gear and improvised housing, had to be taken down, moved and re-erected in Gloucester Valley where the Regiment concentrated. It was some considerable time before order was established and a camp erected. Once this was done, an intensive period of maintenance started and it was only after really getting down to this, that it was appreciated what a truly appalling state a tank gets into after long periods of exposure on hilltops in all sorts of weather and with very little running and maintenance only at night.

Once the tanks were on their feet again, a certain amount of training became possible and all Squadrons took part in Brigade exercises.

Towards the end of February, the weather began to change and the long freeze up showed signs of coming to an end. The snow and the frost gave place to sleet and rain and very quickly the hard dry countryside was converted into a morass. As the frost broke up, the roads caved in under the constant stream of heavily laden traffic and it was not an uncommon sight to see lorries bogged in the middle of the Main Supply Route. To negotiate some of the worst patches, Jeeps had to get into four wheel drive and low box. Frantic efforts by the Corps and Divisional Engineers however, gradually restored them once more to passable routes.

**April 1953**

At the beginning of the month the Commonwealth Division returned to its previous sector of the front. Its deployment was slightly changed as 29 British

Inf. Brigade and 25 Canadian Inf Brigade changed places. This brought 92 Brigade into the left sector with 'C' Squadron in support, 25 Brigade into the central sector with its own Canadian Tank Squadron again in support, 28 Britcom Infantry Brigade returned to the right sector with 'B' Squadron again in support. 'A' Squadron remained in reserve in Gloucester Valley.

The relief went off remarkably smoothly and we found the front little changed, with the exception that enemy shelling and patrolling had increased considerably. It was not uncommon for troop positions to receive up to 200 mixed shells and mortars in the 24 hours.

At first light on 18th April a raid in platoon strength was carried out by troops of 1ROK Division on an enemy-held feature directly in front of the right hand tank of 'B' Squadron which was actually located in the left hand Platoon position of the ROK Division.

Three tanks of 'B' Squadron supported the raid by engaging prearranged targets near the feature and during the raid silenced an enemy machine gun which was firing at the raiding party. During the month the weather improved considerably. The rain stopped and the sun came out, to shine down daily from cloudless skies. It was not long before the spring flowers and shrubs began to come out and soon the dull brown hills were splashed with patches of pink and gold.

**May 1953**

With the advent of the hot weather, activity on all parts of the front increased considerably, both from the point of view of patrolling and shelling.

Major W. D. P. Sullivan took over command of 'C' Squadron, who were still in the line on the left sector, from Major R. E. Maunsell who returned to England on a posting. Major V. J. Senior returned from 444 Forward Delivery Squadron to take over command of HQ Squadron from Major W. D. P. Sullivan.

The month opened with a two-company attack on the night of 2nd May against the 3rd Bn. Royal Canadian Regiment who were holding a part of the front on the central sector. A forward platoon position was overrun but had been restored by first light by a counterattack launched by the reserve company. During this attack, tanks from 'B' Squadron in the Right Brigade sector which had been supporting the Canadians by engaging enemy gun flashes, received heavy harassing fire in return from enemy 122 mm guns.

On 20th May there was a marked increase both in enemy patrolling and shelling on the left sector and it soon became evident that the Chinese were building up for a major attack on the Hook salient which was held by 1st Bn The Duke of Wellington's Regiment with 'C' Squadron in support. Throughout the day of 28th May all tank positions were subjected to heavy shelling by 105 and 122 mm guns, as were all frontline infantry positions in the Hook area. At approximately 8.30 p.m. the Chinese launched their first attacks and were soon engaging the forward infantry positions on the Hook. By 11 p.m. these positions had been captured by the enemy, but after a counterattack by the reserve company they were once more in our hands. In all, four separate attacks were put in on the front of the 'Dukes'. With the exception of the one which gained a temporary footing in the forward position on the Hook, all were halted in front of the FDLs. Throughout the action tanks of 'C' Squadron engaged the enemy and inflicted heavy casualties on them. 504 rounds of 20 pr HE, 22,500 rounds of Besa and 4,500 rounds of Browning were fired.

The tanks themselves averaged five direct hits each from shells and mortars and all tank searchlights were shot out early in the action. It is estimated that during the action 10,000 mixed shells and mortars fell on the forward positions. The enemy casualties were estimated to be 250 killed and 800 wounded, from an attacking force of one Brigade. Although in the right sector where 'B' Squadron were operating no attacks were launched, the front received considerable attention from enemy guns and mortars, Point 159 again taking the brunt. The right hand of the two tanks on Point 159 received a direct hit from an 85 mm AP shot which made a deep gouge on the nose plate but failed to penetrate.

At the end of the month 'A' Squadron, now temporarily commanded by the Second in Command Major H. P. S. Massy, in the absence of Major S. I. Howard Jones on the Coronation Parade, took over from 'B' Squadron in the right Brigade.

**June 1953**

The month opened with celebrations of the Coronation of our Colonel in Chief, Her Majesty Queen Elizabeth II. At 10 o'clock on the morning of Coronation Day the guns of the Divisional Artillery fired a 'Sandwich' of Red, White and Blue smoke onto the Chinese positions. Hardly had the smoke started to thin, when a crashing salvo of one round gun fire rang out, each tank of the Regiment had fired from its battle position at a pre-selected target on the orders of the Commanding Officer. At midday a parade of contingents from all units in the Commonwealth Division was held in the rear areas which was attended by President and Mrs. Synghman Rhee, the Corps Commander Lt Gen Bruce

C. Clark and many other highranking UN Commanders. The Regiment was represented by a troop of highly painted tanks and a dismounted party.

From the point of view of operations, the month was notable for heavy shelling on most positions on the front, 'A' Squadron tanks in the Point 159 and Point 355 areas receiving special attention. Enemy patrols were particularly active in front of Point 159 and patrol clashes in this area resulted in periods of very intensive shelling. On two separate nights the Point 159 position where two tanks were located received approximately 600 mixed shells and mortars inside two hours. It was on one of these occasions that Trooper P. G. Dixon was killed by shell fire while returning from point 159 in a scout car. The shelling also started to stretch further into the rear areas and on two occasions 105 mm shells landed in the area of 'A' Squadron HQ. Towards the end of the month the two right hand tanks of 'A' Squadron assisted in repelling an attack against an outpost to their right front held by the 1st ROK Division. This outpost was a small hill which was completely isolated about 500 yards in front of the FDLs and right out in the middle of no man's land. It was well wired in and held by a force of only 12 ROK soldiers. The pattern of enemy shelling had shown that an attack was likely, so the defensive fire was well laid on. The attack, which, it was later discovered, was of approximately company strength, started shortly after last light, after a heavy bombardment of the outpost and the main line positions supporting it. The weight of the attack resulted in the outpost being rapidly overrun. On the arrival of the Chinese on the position the defenders went to ground in a tunnel, the entrance to which they blocked with sandbags which they maintained in place, in spite of several efforts by the Chinese to blow them in. As soon as the defenders had gone to ground the Divisional Artillery of the 1st ROK Division and the Commonwealth Division was called down on to the position firing VT fuses. To this was added the Besa fire of two tanks and machine gun fire from the infantry main line positions.

The result of this weight of fire on a very small area, was that the Chinese soon retired in considerable disorder. It was estimated that out of an attacking force of 150, they suffered 100 casualties. The next morning the 12 defenders dug themselves out of what was left of their position, slightly dazed but otherwise none the worse for their rather harrowing experience.

On the 'C' Squadron front enemy patrolling remained active and shelling was heavy throughout the month. There were no indications, however, of a build up for a further attack in this area. On the night of 5th

June 'C Squadron supported a raid by 1st Bn. The Kings. At approximately 1 p.m. a large patrol led by an officer crossed the valley with the task of blowing up some caves. The patrol ran into considerable trouble during the night and called for tank fire on several occasions. At 4.30 a.m. they were still on the enemy side of the valley, as a result of which two tanks moved out and covered their withdrawal back in daylight.

**July 1953**

The month opened with the relief of 'C' Squadron by 'B' Squadron in the left sector. This relief was severely hampered by heavy rain and took nine days to complete. Due to the fact that the line in the U.S. Marine Division had been driven back slightly, the Hook area had become an even more pronounced salient than previously and it was therefore decided to move 28 Britcom Inf. Brigade into this sector, as it was the only Brigade. with four Bns. This resulted in a complete switch round of all Brigades. 28 Brigade moved from the right sector to the left; 29 Brigade moved from the central sector to the right sector. To conform with these movements, 'A' Squadron and 'A' Squadron Lord Strathcona's Horse changed places, so that the Strathconas could remain in support of the Canadian Brigade. 'A' Squadron thus found themselves in the central sector. This somewhat tricky manoeuvre was carried out with a remarkable absence of confusion (but not headache) being luckily fitted into a hot dry period between heavy rains. No sooner had the moves been completed than the rains came down heavier than they had ever done before. The River Imjin rose 13 feet in one night and the Commonwealth Division was left with only one Brigade in operation. 'A' and 'B' Squadrons were both cut off as a result of roads being under water and for several days one of 'B' Squadron's troops had to be supplied by 'A' Squadron. Major S. I. Howard Jones returned with the Coronation party towards the end of the month and resumed command of 'A' Squadron shortly after the moves had been completed.

Whilst the Commonwealth Division was indulging in this rather hazardous manoeuvre in the middle of the rainy season and receiving little more attention than its daily dose of shelling, battles were raging furiously on its flanks. On its left in the U.S. Marine Division sector, outposts were falling and being retaken almost nightly. On the right the front was driven in to a considerable depth and restored again after bitter fighting in heavy rain. So strange are the workings of the Oriental mind, that whilst the soldiers of China were being recklessly sacrificed in thousands, her leaders were sitting at the conference table and as the month drew to a close, a truce, so elusive for so long, was unbelievably signed. So the fighting came to an end and as the battle front died into silence, soldiers everywhere emerged from their tanks and bunkers to stand in unaccustomed groups in the defences and gaze across the forbidden valleys at the same strange sight in the enemy lines.

During the last two nights of the war 'B' Squadron came in for a lot of shelling during attacks on adjacent American positions. The two left hand troops from their positions were able to engage the attacking enemy and were in action continuously during both nights, killing a considerable number of enemy and assisting materially in the successful defence of the positions.

During the Korean War the Regiment had had two Squadrons permanently in action for 5 months. In this time it had fired 23,800 rounds from its main armament, received 68 direct hits on its tanks and suffered 20 casualties, one of whom was killed.

All troops were given three days to clear the battlefield of warlike stores and destroy defences, before moving back and leaving a demilitarised zone. These three days were some of the hardest work that the Regiment had had since its arrival in Korea, as there was a vast amount of material to be uprooted and moved. However, the job was completed and the Regiment found itself once more together in Gloucester Valley.

**August and November 1953**

The remainder of the Regiment's time in Korea was spent in constructing a proper camp and digging tank pits and bunkers in the new defence line which would be occupied if the war broke out again. Towards the end of November, during a particularly cold spell, a five day exercise was carried out, during which the new defence line was occupied and defended against powerful hostile attacks which the directing staff conjured up at all hours of the day and night.

At the end of September the Regiment had the melancholy task of saying goodbye to Colonel G. C. Hopkinson, who was returning to England en route to take command of 33 Armoured Brigade in Germany. To him the Regiment owes a very great debt of gratitude, for he above all others was responsible for the Regiment's great success in Korea. He handed over temporary command to Major H. P. S. Massy and it wasn't until the end of November that we were able to welcome our new CO, Colonel N. E. O. Watts, who was flown from England to arrive just in time to take command before the Regiment left Korea. He also fortunately arrived in time to command the Regiment at the Farewell Parade which was attended by the new GOC Major General H. Murray and all the senior officers of the Commonwealth Division. The parade was followed by a lunch party at which over 150 guests were present.

**December 1953**

The Regiment left by train from Tokchon Station at midday on 9th December. At the station to bid us farewell were the GOC Major General H. Murray, the AA and QMG Lt Col JR Fishbourne, Lt Col DW Seaver and Battalion Commanders and other officers of the Commonwealth Division. Also to cheer us on our way were the pipes of the 1st Battalion The Royal Scots and the Band of the 2nd Battalion The Royal Australian Regiment.

The nineteen hour journey to Pusan was completed without incident but in considerable discomfort in an American-run troop train, in which the greatest concession to comfort was a hard wooden seat.

Three days were spent in the Transit Camp in Pusan, during which time the Regiment was kitted out with tropical clothing and handed in its special winter clothing. A Remembrance Service was held in the United Nations cemetery which was attended by the British Minister in Korea and wreaths were laid on the grave of Trooper. P. G. Dixon. Also, a small lunch time cocktail party was held in the Transit Officer's Mess to entertain British Diplomatic Representatives in Korea and the local Commanders and their staffs who helped us with our move.

On 14th December the Regiment embarked on 1 n the *Empire Orwell*, a fine modern troopship run very efficiently by the Orient Line, and very soon we were steaming south, watching the same rugged hills which had welcomed us just one year ago, gradually fading into the past.

Although most of us first learnt of our posting to Korea with mixed feelings, there are few of us who do not look back on it now as a great and valuable experience. We became proficient in an unusual and specialized form of warfare; we met and made friends with many people, not only from all over the Commonwealth, but also from many corners of the world; we lived in a strange and little known country; we fought in a unique and remarkable Army which carries the flags of seventeen nations; and above all we took an active and honourable part in stemming the advance of Communism. It was a year packed with interest, and we took away with us memories which will live for years to come.

# Appendix B

# Order of Battle 1st Royal Tank Regiment December 1952

This is the original published list of Officers who set off to Korea but sadly does not include those who joined us from the Commonwealth once we were 'in station' such as Lt Jack Dutton from South Africa who distinguished himself when he took over my Troop.

**RHQ**

| | | | |
|---|---|---|---|
| CO | Lt Col | GC. | Hopkinson, DSO, MC |
| 2 i/c | Major | HPS. | Massy |
| Adjt | Capt | DVA. | Ambridge, MC |
| A/Adjt | Lieut | MAV. | Rickatson |
| RSO | Lieut | RMH. | Vickers |
| IO | Lieut | TJC. | Cockman |
| RHQ Tp | Lieut | TSM. | Welch |
| LO | Capt | PR. | Wilson |
| RTA | Major | WDP. | Sullivan, MBE |

**HQ SQN**

| | | | |
|---|---|---|---|
| OC | Major | JBB. | Ferguson |
| 2i/c | Capt | SB. | Ferguson |
| RTO | Capt | DG. | Horton |
| PRI | Capt | KC. | Dudley |
| QM | Capt | J. | Taylor, MBE, MM |
| Recce Tp | 2/Lieut | PS. | Berry |
| EME | Capt | WJ. | Exley |
| 2 i/c LAD | Lieut | VV. | O'Shea |
| RMO | Lieut | OP. | Galpin (RAMC) |

ORDER OF BATTLE 1ST ROYAL TANK REGIMENT DECEMBER 1952

| | | | |
|---|---|---|---|
| **A SQN** | | | |
| OC | Major | SI. | Howard Jones, DSO, MC |
| 2 i/c | Capt | JD. | Brotchie, MC |
| | Capt | AE. | Simmons, MC |
| | Lieut | MFV. | Jackson |
| | Lieut | DC. | Crouch |
| | Lieut | PD. | Fanshawe (Bays) |
| | 2/Lieut | PF. | Bede Cox |
| | 2/Lieut | JN. | Busk |
| **B SQN** | | | |
| OC | Major | RE. | Ward, DSO, MC |
| 2 i/c | Major | VJ. | Senior, MC |
| | Capt | AH. | Thrift, MC |
| | Lieut | CGP. | Snowden |
| | Lieut | MH. | Sinnatt |
| | Lieut | MG. | Farmer |
| | Lieut | JA. | Selway |
| | 2/Lieut | M. | Colston (17/21 L) |
| **C SQN** | | | |
| OC | Major | RE. | Maunsell, MC |
| 2 i/c | Capt | RP. | Barker |
| | Capt | JA. | Cowgill |
| | Lieut | AC. | Uloth |
| | 2/Lieut | JD. | Bastick |
| | 2/Lieut | JR. | Chapman |
| | 2/Lieut | SDE. | Lewis |
| **Not initially allocated to Squadrons** | | | |
| | Capt | JPL. | Caunter |
| | Lieut | JDS. | Henderson |
| | Lieut | JB. | Benrum |
| | Lieut | ME. | Roberts |
| | Lieut | G. | Forty |
| | Lieut | R. | Beard |
| | 2/Lieut | PS. | Anthill |
| | 2/Lieut | TJ. | Thomas |
| | 2/Lieut | JL. | Damant (7th H) |